EARLY ENCOUNTERS WITH CHILDREN AND ADOLESCENTS

Early Encounters with Children and Adolescents is the first training guide to use the works of beginning therapists as its focus. Far too often, therapists in training are given the "classics" to read—case histories by the masters in the field, which can sometimes leave beginning therapists intimidated or even in despair as to whether they can ever reach that level of proficiency. This book is the first to remediate that situation by providing beginners with role models they can more easily internalize through realistic case histories that reveal the ins and outs of starting in a craft that is never fully mastered. Not only are the cases themselves fascinating, but the therapists also refer to the processes they struggled with while treating these patients. Readers will thus have a striking new counterweight to the classics they will still want to read as they progress in the field. Eight beginning clinicians discuss aspects of their clinical process, including: issues of transference and countertransference; the role of supervision; doing parent consultations, especially when one is not yet a parent; cultural, racial, and socioeconomic differences between patient and therapist; and the vulnerability of not understanding for long moments in treatment. Psychodynamic beginners in every discipline will find these case histories compelling, heartfelt, and inspiring.

Steven Tuber, PhD, ABPP, is professor of psychology and director of clinical training in the doctoral program in clinical psychology at the City College of New York, where he has taught for nearly 30 years. He is the author of three critically acclaimed books: *Attachment, Play, and Authenticity: A Winnicott Primer* (2008), *Starting Treatment with Children and Adolescents* (2011), and *Understanding Personality Through Projective Testing* (2012).

EARLY ENCOUNTERS WITH CHILDREN AND ADOLESCENTS

Beginning Psychodynamic Therapists' First Cases

Edited by Steven Tuber

Routledge
Taylor & Francis Group

NEW YORK AND LONDON

First published 2015
by Routledge
711 Third Avenue, New York, NY 10017

and by Routledge
27 Church Road, Hove, East Sussex BN3 2FA

Routledge is an imprint of the Taylor & Francis Group, an informa business

Library of Congress Cataloging-in-Publication Data
Early encounters with children and adolescents: beginning psychodynamic therapists' first cases/[edited] by Steven Tuber.
p.; cm.
Eight of these ten chapters have been previously published in a modified version by Routledge in the December 2013 edition of the Journal of infant, child and adolescent psychotherapy (JICAP, volume 12).
Includes bibliographical references and index.
I. Tuber, Steven, 1954-, editor. II. Journal of infant, child and adolescent psychotherapy.
[DNLM: 1. Child. 2. Psychotherapy, Psychodynamic—Case Reports.
3. Psychotherapy, Psychodynamic—Collected Works. 4. Adolescent. WS 350.2]
RJ505.P92
618.92'8914—dc23
2014030556

ISBN: 978-1-138-81591-9 (hbk)
ISBN: 978-1-138-81592-6 (pbk)
ISBN: 978-1-315-74650-0 (ebk)

Typeset in Bembo
by Swales and Willis Ltd., Exeter, Devon, UK

Printed and bound in the United States of America by Publishers Graphics, LLC on sustainably sourced paper.

To all beginning therapists, we welcome you warmly to a most noble profession.

CONTENTS

CONTRIBUTORS

Elizabeth Freidin Baumann, PhD

Zoë Berko, MPhil

Kira Boesch, MA

Monique S. Bowen, PhD

Jane Caflisch, PhD

Lauren DeMille, PhD

Jenny Kahn Kaufmann, PhD

Jason Royal, PhD

Steven Tuber, PhD, ABPP

Mougeh Yasai, PhD

1

AN INTRODUCTION

Steven Tuber

This book emerges from the vantage point of having educated doctoral students in clinical psychology for over thirty years. A question that has taken up a great deal of my pedagogical time and thought has been: how best does a beginning child therapist learn to be a competent clinician? I think there are three sources of learning. First and foremost, clinicians at any level, but especially beginners, learn most from their patients; there is no substitute for actual clinical experience. Second, students learn from their supervisors; there is little that can match the role that modeling and insight play in developing a beginning therapist. Third, students learn from what they read. Reading in child/adolescent psychotherapy, moreover, has historically taken one of two forms. The first form is the paradigm whereby a master clinician writes a book that provides conceptual understanding of specific personality issues and/or adds clinical case vignettes to support her work. Classics in this genre by such authors as Anna Freud, Melanie Klein, Donald Winnicott, Virginia Axline and Clark Moustakas were read when I was a student in the 1970s and are still read today.

The second form such books take are "how to" books, guiding the neophyte step by step from the first phone call with the parents through the evaluation process and eventual treatment of the child, including practical information on how to set up a therapy room, set limits etc. This type of work, epitomized by the works of Lanyado, Brumfield and Blake, is also essential to the training of any good child psychotherapist.

There is something missing, however, from both of these forms of required reading for beginners. Both these types of books have been written by "experts" in the field, putting the beginner in an especially difficult quandary: how to bridge the gap between these "pearls of wisdom" and the present state of fragility and vulnerability that the new therapist commonly feels. I have often felt that a long-standing deficiency, particularly within the arena of the training of psychodynamically informed clinicians, has been the near exclusive reliance on conceptual and clinical writings from the "masters" within our field. This certainly makes sense regarding conceptual additions to our development. It does take years of clinical craftsmanship, observation and thinking across a wide variety of settings before nuanced contributions to the how and why of health and pathology can be added to the literature. But when it comes to clinical cases, I don't think this is nearly as true. The gap between the typical, usually highly successful process and outcome of a case presented by a senior clinician and the day-to-day strivings of a novice therapist is cavernous. I argue that this "gap" can be closed somewhat by hearing directly from beginning therapists themselves. Having such beginners speak not only to the clinical content of their cases, but to add in their experience of the process of being a beginner can be an invaluable addition to their training. This gap, moreover, while certainly providing something for the beginner to strive toward closing, is equally likely to evoke feelings of inadequacy, if not self-castigation or even despair. Perhaps more deadly, it may evoke a false self persona in the budding therapist: a far too complete assimilation of what they think they are supposed to think, act and feel like when with a child patient, and a concomitant need to disown feelings of vulnerability. This not only runs the risk of interfering with their capacity to be with their patients in the consulting room, at its worst, it also initiates a false dialogue in the supervisory process, whereby a loss of authenticity to be dreaded by all in the field may ensue. This is especially true when process notes as opposed to verbatim recordings are used as the sole source of data in the supervisory process. Selective remembering of the treatment process, on both a conscious and unconscious level, can distort the training of the trainee and limit both their and their patient's development.

While these phenomena are always at play in our training, they can be reduced by two major factors. One is of course the talent of the supervisor/teacher to create a milieu of trust and openness in the supervisory and academic settings respectively. This is indeed an absolute necessity for the optimal development of any clinician. But another important factor is the role peers play in providing an arena where the safe admission of ignorance, clumsiness and/or "blindness" can be tacitly relied upon. Hearing the "mistakes" of one's peers emboldens a student therapist to admit their own foibles. Getting benign, constructive feedback from a supervisor in the presence of one's peers, or perhaps equally useful feedback from the peers themselves, whether in the classroom, the group supervision or the student "lounge," hastens the development of an ego-driven comfort with one's presence with patients, as opposed to a superego-laden vision of what one is supposed to be like. The intrinsic abundance of anxiety that is inexorable in the first months and years with patients can and is mitigated by the knowledge that your peers are not much better off than you are. When this peer influence is combined with the help of seasoned supervisors, the growth curve is accelerated to the betterment of trainee, patient and supervisor.

This edited volume can therefore be seen as an extension of the role of peer contributions in one's clinical training to the realm of the written word. Eight present or recently graduated students from a psychodynamically informed doctoral program in clinical psychology were invited to write up either their very first or one of their very first long-term child cases. They were asked to depict their work with an eye toward their own process of development as the case unfolded. Issues of transference and countertransference; cultural differences between patient and therapist; despair and frustration when changes were not forthcoming; vulnerability when the patient is not understood; inadequacies regarding dealing with parents, especially when one is not yet a parent; the vicissitudes of help or the lack thereof from supervisors: all these are courageously and honestly detailed.

It is especially notable that almost all of the cases described in this volume ended "prematurely." That is, either the parent of the patient withdrew the child from treatment abruptly, often without notice (see Chapters 7, 8, 9 and 10); or the therapist terminated the case because their training at that particular institution had ended (see Chapters 3 and 4). This phenomenon occurs so regularly in the lives of clinicians at training clinics, and yet is so rarely discussed, that it takes on the quality of a "dirty little secret" that nearly all clinicians experience yet rarely, if ever, discuss in a public forum. This book bucks this trend by not only selecting cases that do end this way, but in its poignant discussion of what this feels like to the beginning therapist.

It is the fondest wish of the editor and contributors to this volume that the cases about to be described prove to be of much use to trainees and beginning clinicians across the disciplines of psychology, psychiatry and social work. We also hope that in addition to the benefits that trainees may derive from the book, their supervisors in these disciplines will also derive utility from hearing how trainees experience their first cases. Some of these case presentations were first published in slightly different form in the December 2013 issue of the *Journal of Infant, Child and Adolescent Psychotherapy* (JICAP). JICAP had generously allowed me to not only edit those original presentations for that "special issue," but to provide a periodic, ongoing forum for such case presentations. It is hoped that with that forum, coupled with the present edited volume, we will be well on the way to providing a consistent third source of readings for beginning clinicians.

The eight cases to be presented are quite varied, both in terms of the child's presenting problems and the particular patient-therapist process that transpired. The first case (Chapter 2) is entitled: "The Very First Patient: Becoming Real Together" and is written by Kira Boesch. Here Kira presents literally her first patient, indeed, as she puts it, for the first months of Evan's treatment, he was her first and only patient. Evan's play therapy is ongoing, with no upcoming termination issues to wrestle with for at least another year or two. Here the presentation focuses on the raw newness of the experience of being a therapist for the first time, and trying to find a language and way of being that works with her patient.

The child's almost immediate intense connection to the therapist, epitomized by his creation of a doll he calls "Kira," stirred up very powerful issues in the therapist's evolving comfort with being called a therapist and feeling authentic in that process. This chapter thus provides a compelling means of hearing how a new therapist negotiates what therapy can mean to a child. It also provides a window into the processes of symbolization in play vs. concrete and literal enactment and this shift in interaction is a constant theme of the treatment. How to handle the intense transference and countertransference aspects of this doll play makes this case especially evocative and useful.

Mougeh Yasai's (Chapter 3) work with a 12 year-old girl and her 31 year-old mom provides a dyadic treatment format with which beginning child therapists often must wrestle. The chapter is entitled "How Do I Work With Parent *and* Child, Especially if I Am Not Yet a Parent?" One extremely common aspect of child/adolescent therapy that is rarely discussed is how a childless therapist can provide both parental guidance and astute child work when she or he has never been a parent. Yasai bravely confronts this issue head-on, tolerating her own anxieties and discomforts as she builds faith in her clinical prowess and process over a three-year long treatment. She is repeatedly courageous and clear in her depictions of her self-doubt and of the complex levels of interaction among patient, mother, therapist and supervisor as they struggle together with the difficult issues raised by the work. In particular, issues of differences in culture and social class between mother and therapist are described with subtlety and nuance.

Elizabeth Baumann (in Chapter 4) then writes her depiction of the case of William, a seven year-old boy with a chronic history of loss and neglect. Chapter 4 is entitled: "How Do I Work Long-Term With a Child When I Only Have a Year to Work With Him?" Through the use of a play therapy drawing technique, she finds a meaningful and poignant method of entering this child's inner world. Given this boy's history, a central aspect of the case is Liz's knowing that she can only treat him until her one-year Internship ends. Literally every trainee across the psychiatric disciplines is faced with the crucial question Baumann poses. Training in our field inevitably involves an Internship or Practicum experience in which the child's need for ongoing treatment is at odds with the limited amount of time the trainee is at a given institution. The feelings of loss and guilt that termination imposes when it is the therapist who has to leave first is poignantly described in this chapter and is certain to evoke powerful resonance with readers who are entering the field. This in and of itself is a prominent and often neglected aspect of the literature on training psychodynamically informed clinicians: the degree to which the termination process is determined not by the patient's progress but by the time-limited nature of the therapist's clinical setting. Liz speaks beautifully to the pain and poignancy of the termination process between herself and William, as well as the impact of various supervisory and academic experiences she had that influenced her work.

The book takes a slight shift at this point with the back-to-back chapters of a beginning therapist and her supervisor writing about an adolescent case. Monique Bowen (Chapter 5) presents her work with Aden, a 19 year-old college student. Chapter 5 is entitled: "Finding One's Self: Developing a Therapeutic Identity as a Beginning Therapist Doing Long-Term Work." This chapter amplifies the preceding chapters in its focus on monitoring the growth of the therapist over time in fostering a sense of personal authenticity while doing this work. It also is more specific in its brave focus on "mistakes" made by the therapist, mistakes which over time serve to aid in the development of both therapist and patient.

Three issues not previously focused upon in the three previous cases assume center stage here. First, the issue of the patient's immigration to the US, its comparisons with the therapist's father's immigration experience and the countertransferential themes evoked by their similarities and differences are described. Racial and ethnic differences between patient and therapist also play a profound part of this treatment process and are described here. Of interest also is the third issue of the therapist's open acknowledgement, first to her supervisor and then to us, of the role her reveries about her patient, both in and out of the session, play in the treatment process.

In the next chapter (6), Monique's supervisor on the case, Jenny Kaufmann, provides a wonderful portrait of her experience with the case, granting us a window into the triad of patient-therapist-supervisor that we rarely see in print. Her chapter is entitled: "Modeling a Therapeutic Identity for a Beginning Therapist in Supervision." Here the author revisits the supervisory relationship's formative function in the professional development of the trainee. Of special emphasis are the roles culture, privilege and race play in the triad of patient-therapist-supervisor, as all three persons are of different racial, class and ethnic backgrounds.

Chapter 7, entitled: "Building Safety and Containment: Responding to Challenges to the Frame With Both Parent and Child" is written by Jane Caflisch. Here Jane describes her work with a boy who was dealing with severe separation issues, fomented in large part by an unspoken, significant, chronic medical illness of his mother, an illness whose multiple layers including a marked instability regarding the treatment appointments themselves. At many points in the treatment, the symptoms he presented and his erratic attendance forced Jane to face a challenge many other beginners have to face: how do you prioritize whether the parent or the child is most in need of treatment, especially when dyadic treatment is not accepted by the parent?

Chapter 8, called: " 'Following the Affect': How My First Child Patient Helped Teach Me to Listen and See" is written by Jason Royal. Here the author takes on yet another formidable obstacle to beginning work with children, especially young children. The patient is a five year-old boy and his symbolic play is confusing and chaotic much of the time. How the therapist learns to follow the child's feeling states despite and sometimes because of the chaos his play creates is thoughtfully depicted. Indeed, in my experience teaching therapy all these years, helping the beginner not get overwhelmed by the non-linear, sometimes nonsensical, mind of a young child is crucial to his or her becoming an effective clinician.

The last two cases to be presented provide a most unusual situation: two therapists describe their work with the same adolescent patient over the course of their successive Internship placements at the same site. Chapters 9 and 10 are thus entitled: "'Psychic Twins': a Psycho-dynamically Informed Treatment of a Selectively Mute Adolescent and Her Mother" and "Passing the Baton From One Beginning Therapist to the Next: an Adolescent Treated by Two Successive Interns" written by Zoë Berko and Lauren DeMille. These two chapters provide the reader with a most unusual phenomenon. Two therapists, each working in their Internship year, happen to be placed, one year after the other, in the same treatment center, where they are assigned the same treatment case. The patient, a selectively mute adolescent girl, thus provides us with a treatment from two vantage points. During the first year of her treatment, the issues explored in the previous chapters are again manifest. The second year of treatment, moreover, provides the reader with a paradigm that commonly occurs in the course of psychotherapy training; namely that of dealing with the complex issues involved in taking on a case transferred from a previous therapist. Issues of competition and comparison are difficult for any therapist to wrestle with, but are exceptionally germane to the trials and tribulations of being a beginning therapist.

Zoë Berko began the treatment of 18 year-old "J," a selective mute and her "psychic twin" mother in a dyadic format. The unique vicissitudes of this remarkable symptom and its impact on her, her family and on the therapist are beautifully rendered. When Lauren DeMille, a colleague of Zoë's from the same Doctoral Program in Clinical Psychology, takes over the case after a year of treatment by Zoë, we are given a chance to see the impact of termination in a different light. We are also provided a meaningful glimpse into the assets, doubts and vulnerabilities involved in taking over a case from a prior trainee. Lauren is able to take the gains made by J with Zoë and use them to expand the treatment to both individual and dyadic work, leading to the remarkable moment when J utters her first words outside the home in years.

Eight of these ten chapters have already been published in a modified version by Routledge in the December 2013 edition of the *Journal of Infant, Child and Adolescent Psychotherapy* (JICAP, Volume 12). I would like to thank Dr. Susan Warshaw, Editor in Chief of JICAP, for her kind permission to publish these slightly differing versions of these articles in book form. Wherever possible, the consent of the parents and assent of the child were garnered before publication. When this was not feasible, the demographic material for these families has been heavily disguised without misrepresenting the core work of each case.

2

THE VERY FIRST PATIENT

Becoming Real Together

Kira Boesch

Evan was my first patient. He was turning eight when we began working together. He is now ten, and the treatment is ongoing.

Evan was raised by both of his parents until he was school-aged, at which point he revealed to a mandated reporter that his mother beat him. Child Protective Services was called, and that agency removed Evan from his family home a few days later. Evan spent the better part of a year with a distant family member before being returned to the custody of his father. He was allowed supervised visits with his mother.

Evan's father sought treatment for his son because in the year prior to our beginning treatment Evan had been having "fits of anger." In response to being teased, Evan would quickly become tremendously upset and begin hitting himself and screaming. Sometimes he would express suicidal ideas. On two occasions when this happened at school, it landed him in the psychiatric Emergency Room. Evan's father also sought treatment for Evan because of his understanding of the likely depth of the repercussions resulting from Evan's early and extended trauma.

When I met Evan for the first time, his anxiety and fear were palpable, as was his need to cover them with a forced confidence and illusion of control. Tuber (2008), in his discussion of Winnicott's paper, "Communicating and Not Communicating Leading to a Study of Certain Opposites," (1963), discusses Winnicott's idea that in malignant rearing environments, the growing infant must show a false or compliant self to the other, forcing the real or true self to become hidden in order to be preserved. I saw much of Evan's compliant self in our first two sessions. On the first day, he walked straight over to the small table in the therapy room. Plopping into one of the chairs he sighed, "Okay, I'm ready. What do you want me to do?" Evan ultimately ended up "playing" teacher during that session, although there was little playfulness to it. Instead, Evan impersonated his teacher with uncanny accuracy. In our second session, Evan recreated the first session with precision, almost as if it were his job to do so.

The first two sessions just described took place within a room with a two-way mirror through which others could observe. I imagined that this might be difficult for Evan, whose experiences of revealing things to professionals in the past had had the consequences of his being removed from his home by Child Protective Services and trips to the hospital Emergency Room. Indeed, Evan seemed not to lose awareness of the presence of our audience for even a second as he acted out his teacher performance, intermittently turning to the mirror to wave with dramatized enthusiasm. Later he would call that room "the room with the spies." I was given only a brief glimpse of Evan's real self while we met in that room, when, at the very end of his second session, Evan approached the shelf farthest from the mirror. Facing away from our audience, he reached directly for a Barbie doll in one of the toy bins. He borrowed the hair elastic on my wrist to style her hair, and as he passed it back to me, I had my first feeling of connection to Evan.

Evan and I ultimately settled into a very small therapy room with no mirror and no windows. Evan had immediately become enamored with our room the first time we had a session there, when he discovered that it had "an elevator" in it—a large empty metal cabinet with a sliding door that Evan could climb in and out of, shielding him from my view temporarily. It was in this room, often hidden from view, that Evan revealed parts of his real self over time. Our relationship began to take shape within this lived dialectic between hiding and showing and real and false.

I have seen Evan twice a week for over a year now. Our relationship and our world have been created within this small room of his choosing. In the beginning, it felt very much as if there were no space in that room—no space for thinking about feelings, and no space for us to coexist naturally and comfortably with one another, sometimes in silence. As time has gone on we have created, together, a little bit of breathing room. There has been a parallel process as Evan has increasingly allowed his real self and real feelings to emerge into our relationship at the same time that I have come to know myself in this new role as his therapist and to feel more authentic in that role.

When Evan and I started to work together, I lacked the experience to know what the process of therapy would entail. Both our relationship and our process originated with us reacting to one another. I was learning by doing, and I think both because of the nature of therapy and of any new endeavor, that largely meant watching and responding to Evan's words and actions. Evan is a keen and vigilant observer of the other, such that as I reacted to him, it often felt as though he was effortfully defining himself in reaction to me as well. "What's her name?" he would ask me about a pretend character. "What should her job be? How old do you think she is?" He was loath to decide anything without my input. It was as if Evan had a need to know what I thought and felt in order to feel safe; he did not have the luxury of assuming that the content of my mind was benign. I could easily envision that molding his compliant self to others' wants had developed as a survival skill. At the same time, early sessions were also replete with a different, less direct, and less compliant mode of communication. What Evan could not yet tell me, he showed me. Ever since that brief moment of finding the Barbie doll, Evan created pretend play scenarios with her while I simply observed. In turn, I grew to feel more authentic as a child therapist by seeing myself in that role reflected back at me from Evan's experience.

The Frame of the Pretend World

The Protagonist

One month into the treatment Evan named his Barbie doll character "Kira." As soon as she was named Kira she was also given the role of mother. Each session since has revolved around Kira and her family. Upon entering the room Evan immediately finds his Barbie doll, often expressing his need for continuity out loud, saying things like, "I hope she's where I left her," or "I hope nobody changed her hairstyle." At times Evan has Kira interact with her children or other members of her family—her husband, her sister-in-law, her father or her mother. Other times it is all about her; but the frame of Kira and her family remains. When he does not wish to play with the children, Evan makes sure to state that they are in Puerto Rico visiting their grandmother, and often decides in advance when they will return.

In early sessions I was an observer only, often in the position of simply witnessing as Evan had Kira alternating between being solicitously sweet and abusive toward her children. I commented on what I was seeing unfold, noticing, for example, when it seemed as though the doll child being screamed at, hit, or thrown across the room had not actually done anything wrong. In response to my comments, Evan jerked his head around, simultaneously twisting his doll's head and saying, "Am I hearing voices? Who is that? Are they following me?" I played along, using a doll to embody my voice. Evan had his doll confront mine, furious at first. A moment later he had his doll, Kira, invite my new character to come to dinner, and then to be her son's godmother. Evan did not want me on the outside looking in, and from that moment onward I was in the play, first as Kira's children's godmother, and a few months later until the present, as her sister. It is quite a conflict for Evan to be seen by me. Even now, the space for me to comment on Evan's play or experience frequently feels elusive. I imagine that by having me in the play, as his sister, as part of his family, he can better tolerate the real me observing his experience from the outside. Evan's relationship to being seen is a key aspect of his treatment, and will be revisited in later sections of this chapter.

Hair

Much of the play has revolved, and continues to revolve, around the act of doing the characters' hair. At first, Evan did Kira's hair privately, often seeming to shape the play around reasons for him to get into the "elevator" where he would style her hair repeatedly while hidden from my view. Later, Evan came to do her hair outside of the elevator, but still seemed to shape the play around it, such that Kira was constantly getting ready for one activity or another. Eventually, Evan made Kira a pop star and model, such that the act of doing her hair for her shows became more explicit as a goal of the play. Sometimes, Evan will wistfully say, "I wish we could just do hair," and more and more he is occasionally able to simply announce that that is what we will be doing. He still grounds this in the play story, however, saying that Kira is getting ready for a show that will not happen until our next session.

The activity of doing hair has allowed different aspects of Evan to enter the room. Mostly, Evan will pretend that he is Kira, the Barbie doll, doing her own hair. This allows him to play out some of his feminine identifications and wishes. Sometimes, however, Evan pretends that Kira has gone to the hair salon where she can get her hair done professionally by stylist Evan, and he can enjoy being male and himself while doing elaborate hair-dos at the same time. Finally, the activity of doing hair is what has allowed Evan to sometimes talk to me directly, as himself, rather than as a character. It was many months before this occurred, and to this day Evan seems uncomfortable talking to me directly. More and more, however, if there is something on his mind, it will reach the air between us, and without fail, this will occur while Evan is busily braiding Kira's hair. He will begin to tell me about things by way of keeping me informed, feigning a casual attitude. "Oh did I tell you what happened the other day? I got teased. I hate teasing." He drops these nuggets of raw facts into the air, heavily. I try to keep the heavy ball in the air, rather than letting it thud to the ground, asking follow-up questions and expressing my genuine interest in knowing about how Evan is thinking and feeling. Usually after a short back and forth Evan clips in, "Should I wear the blue shoes?" and it takes a moment for me to realize that he has become Kira again. It is as if it becomes too much for him to be so exposed as the direct topic of conversation, and he quickly brings our interaction back to the pretend realm.

Last but not least, the emphasis on hair in our sessions has given Evan a forum for addressing our racial differences. As he imbues his play character with some of my characteristics, Evan seems to be painfully aware of the ways in which he differs in appearance from me. Evan talks about coveting thin and straight hair like mine, and despising his own thick and curly hair. He talks about the characters doing their hair in styles that are particular to his Latino cultural group, saying, "You don't know how to do that style, do you?" Beneath his outermost envy, there is also a sense of pride of his heritage, and an understandable probing on his part that seems to derive from a place of wondering what I know about his cultural group and, more fundamentally, whether I can understand him and where he is coming from.

The Invisible Audience

The audience came into existence during a brief period in which I was recording my sessions with Evan for my training purposes. Evan, in his inimitable fashion, essentially expressed that he felt intruded upon by a mysterious audience in the session before I began recording, even though I had not yet told him about the recording. When I did begin to record our sessions, Evan was (and by extension, I was too) deeply thrown by the intrusion, and he communicated to me in gestures and mouthed words (so that the recording could not hear) that he felt "freaked out."

At first, the presence of the audience may have been Evan's way of mastering the experience of being listened to and "watched" by my tape recorder and the audience it represented to him. However, the audience has remained a fixture of our pretend frame and seems to have provided, so to speak, a necessary stage upon which various conflicts can be played out. If the real audience that observed our first two sessions resulted in Evan feeling the need to hide his real self, the pretend audience creates another way for some of his real feelings to come to light.

The presence of the audience draws an invisible curtain around Evan and me, which, when closed, shields us from the view of others. Rather than my being the observing therapist looking in at him, Evan has placed me with him on the stage before the invisible audience. At the same time, the audience also allows for Evan to engage with not only his fears but also his wishes to exhibit himself, to be seen and admired.

As Evan shifts between identifying with Kira, the model, and with the audience, he can experience himself as being observed and simultaneously place himself into the stance of the observer. Themes of deprivation are never far from the surface. When Evan announces that we will just be doing hair rather than modeling, something he seems to really want, he nevertheless has the invisible and ever-present "audience" complain bitterly that they will not see Kira. "We bought tickets, we paid money, we came all the way here!" he has the audience gripe. In large part, I believe that Evan identifies with the audience, wanting more time with this mother character. She is never there as much as the audience wants her to be. This speaks to Evan's experience both of his real mother and of me in the transference.

Evan can start to master this experience by also identifying as Kira—as both me and his mother at once. In this complementary role he gets to do the depriving, to be the one who leaves and leaves others wanting more. He is in control of when the hungry audience gets to see Kira and when they do not. At the same time he receives the careful watching, the attention, and the adoration from the audience that he may have received only haphazardly and unreliably from his real mother.

Variations Within the Frame

While Evan keeps each session very much the same as the last, there is notable fluidity in Evan's play when it comes to choosing a doll to represent the character of "Kira." As the treatment has continued, we have acquired more dolls to choose from. We have always had some dolls that resemble Caucasian women and some that look more like Latina women. Evan often starts sessions by wondering aloud, "who should I be today?" As such, while Evan's character Kira is an absolute constant in every session, her appearance is ever changing, and along with it her race and hair texture. By keeping Kira's appearance fluid Evan can go back and forth between a Kira that resembles me and one that has more of the physical characteristics of his real mother, keeping her a combination of multiple representations. This stance is consistent with Evan's fluid gender identity—his choice to spend some of the session as a female character and some as his own male self.

Themes of Treatment

Merging

At the core of Evan's experience of himself and others, and similarly of others' experience of him, is his unintegrated sense of self and diffuse identity. Evan has great difficulty creating a boundary between us as separate people in contact with one another. For several months early on, Evan would talk for my character, or for the children, whose voices he had assigned to me. He was Kira, I was Kira, and he would overflow into being my play characters as well, usually without noticing until I brought it to his attention. Even the way my character entered the play was through a merging of minds; my character started out inside of Evan's character's head, in the form of voices she heard.

A major theme of our treatment has revolved around Evan's fantasied merger with me. Evan wanted to become me in the play. He borrowed the extra rubber bands I always had on my wrist to use in Kira's hair. He borrowed my keys and put them in Kira's purse pretending they were hers. During our first year of working together I became engaged to be married, and Evan was concerned that I had only an engagement ring and not a wedding ring. Thereafter he introduced Kira's husband into the play, and staged much marital strife owing to the fact that Kira could never seem to find her wedding ring. As Evan became more able to create solid boundaries around himself, his play character, me, and my play character, he began to merge with me in far more subtle ways. One day, when I was wearing tall boots for the first time in a session of ours, Evan, wearing his usual short boots, complained that he was having a very hard time sitting that day in his tall boots.

Early on, I struggled with Evan's need to infuse our pretend play with aspects of my real life. I was trying desperately to establish myself as a therapist and to navigate the boundaries associated with that new role. Those fragile boundaries felt threatened by Evan asking me for my middle name, my husband's name, and my home address so that he could apply them to the play. Looking back, I think another part of my difficulty with this aspect of the treatment was that it forced me to set limits. It felt overwhelming to say no to Evan, and to tell him that I was not going to give him the answers to all of his questions. I could not ignore that from his perspective these limits would seem ridiculous, impossible to explain, and rejecting. I think it was part of my not having found my voice as a therapist that contributed to my finding this part of the treatment hard; I could not yet balance my understanding of Evan's perspective with a solid perspective of my own that I could easily call upon while with Evan. In retrospect, I think I also sensed Evan's strong feelings of being deprived by me whenever I did not provide him with the information he wanted. It was yet another way in which I resisted Evan experiencing me as withholding. I now recognize that this was part of the negative transference that was beginning to emerge, and luckily, I received the support I needed in supervision to allow it to do so before too long.

From a theoretical standpoint, Evan's desire for merger with me in the play was partly a product of his traumatic past. Tuber and Coates (1985) suggest that boys who behave in feminine ways often have had real or psychical separations from their mothers. Tuber and Coates (1985) note that these boys may attempt to behave like their mother as a means of maintaining an internal tie to her, confusing having mommy with being mommy. Importantly, the primitive idealization and identification in which the boys engage leads to the development of a false self and a distorted representation of both self and other. Consistent with this theoretical stance, I felt as though Evan was trying to identify with and merge with me as his only means of relating.

Slowly, Evan freed his representation of Kira from the tight constraints around her having to be like me. This change appeared in many aspects of Kira, including her job. At first Kira was a camp counselor, a professional working with children. Now she is a model and actress, a job more directly influenced by Evan's fantasies and wishes. Evan's use of different dolls to represent Kira can also be seen as a manifestation of his taking more ownership of who she is and allowing her to be what and who he wants her to be. Importantly, as Evan's character became more him and less me, it helped him to see me as separate from him. This opened up his ability to internalize me as a benign and caring adult in his life, but also to see me as a depriving and rejecting figure in the transference.

As Evan does hair, he often asks me to hand him the hair supplies he needs. In earlier sessions he would say, "I need . . . never mind, I'll get it myself." It felt like progress when he began to order me around somewhat, saying, "Oh and I need a rubber band," or "Yeah, I'm going to need a few more of those bobby pins." These are moments of easy connection, and we talk as I provide what he needs for Kira's hair. Nevertheless, there are other times when Evan still apologizes when he asks me to pass him things and I now recognize that in these moments Evan is viewing me through his transference as unable to supply what he needs. In these other kinds of moments, Evan tells me outright, not as a belief but as reality, that I must prefer to do something else, that just sitting there passing him hairpins is not what I really want to be doing. In these latter moments, Evan's projections of internalized self-hatred are mine to contain. As Evan becomes more able to internalize me as a benign provider, he will be more able to see me as separate but non-threatening.

Wanting and Needing More

It has been a journey in the treatment to get to a place where Evan can express his feelings of being deprived by me in a more direct way. When we first began working together, few if any of Evan's feelings were accessible to him in symbolized form. He could not tell me about his feelings, or even name them, instead finding ways to show me his feelings.

At the start of treatment, Evan noticed everything out of place or unclean in the therapy room. "Why is this here?" he would mumble about some small piece of garbage, adding, "I'll just throw it out later." He would sometimes, and still does, hurt himself in the room, knocking his elbow or his head against the "elevator" as though by accident. Evan often complains of a backache, and squirms around, showing me that he cannot be physically comfortable. In these moments his frustration, pain and discomfort are there to be seen, experienced and narrated by me, without the distance that symbolized representation would provide. His feelings take on a global nature fitting with Thompson's (1986) most primitive level of affect maturity in which emotions have a mood-like quality and are tied to the atmosphere in general rather than to the self or other.

Many of the negative feelings Evan conveys are around the issue of wanting and needing more, as exemplified by his commentary as the pretend audience described above. Through the expression of these feelings Evan simultaneously shows me that I am important to him, and also that he experiences me as not providing enough. During his very first session, Evan asked what days and times we would be meeting, why he was not coming back the following week instead of in two weeks, and whether some of the other rooms had more chalk. Since then, Evan has expressed a desire for *more* in almost every session—mostly focused around more time with me. "We only get fifty minutes? I thought we got an hour?" he will say periodically. Other times, he will ask why we cannot end our session late given that he arrived late. Every so often Evan asks, "Why don't I come three days not just two?" Sometimes, he accepts all of these realities, and can begin to take ownership of his feelings, saying things like "I need all my minutes." In expressing his desire for more therapy and more of my time, Evan also communicates to me his very real experience of not getting enough. There seems to be rarely a moment that Evan does not feel the effects of his having been neglected by the very person who was supposed to care for him.

The therapeutic frame confronts Evan with his conflict about being seen. He desperately wants and needs to be seen and listened to in a way that he missed having enough of as an infant and young child. At the same time, he is terrified of being seen and heard. I often wonder what the beginning of treatment would have looked like if not for the elevator. The elevator created a place where Evan could avoid being looked at by me at the same time that he showed me what he needed me to know. It was in the elevator, shielded from my view, that Evan first began to act out Kira verbally abusing her children. It was also there, as mentioned above, that he first began to style Kira's hair. Slowly but steadily Evan brought these behaviors and aspects of his internal life out of the elevator. His vulnerability in doing so was clear. If we heard voices or footsteps in the hallway, Evan would look at me wide-eyed, asking anxiously if we could be heard by those outside the room.

While Evan's questioning of who can hear or see him may be intermittent, his play around the theme of being seen and heard is constant. The ever-present invisible audience guarantees this. Winnicott, as presented by Tuber (2008), might describe Evan's conflict around being seen in terms of the terrifying need to be found, and the equally terrifying potentiality of not being found. As Tuber (2008) puts it, Evan wants to be known, but not owned. At the same time, Evan's fear of being found may join forces with his real and understandable persecutory fears. Fonagy et al. (2002) write of the avoidance of finding oneself in the other's mind in instances of relational trauma in which what there is to be found may well be threatening.

een, may also be so significant for Evan because he acts as
d inside of a person must match. Kira looks messy when
ust look good because she is good. This line of thinking
s into the treatment, and is representative of Thompson's
affect maturity. At this level, emotions are attributed on
tures, and are still thought of more as events than as psy-

rtunity to think about his internal states may be partly
ssed level of affect maturity. For Evan, his feelings have
vn, such that they actually are on the outside before he
comes aware that he is angry only when he sees him-
counts somewhat for Evan's acute sensitivity to being
or say they see) in Evan becomes *the* reality. In the room
starting to distinguish what is seen from what is real.
nt he had a character act very happy and excited and
my real self." Indeed, neither he nor his character was

believably happy in that moment, despite appearing, or acting, to the contrary. More recently, Evan pretends that his character is wearing a wig or hair extensions, but that the audience naively believes it is real hair.

As Evan plays with the idea of real hair, and selves, being seen and hidden, some of his deepest preoccupations are given space in which to be mastered. As Tuber (2008) elucidates, it is play in a benign and reliable environment that helps the growing child master the separation of "me" and "not me." In turn, the real self connotes a sense of distinction, of separateness from the other. As Evan plays, he is developing a real self, separate from his character Kira, and separate from the representations of me and his mother that are bound up in her.

The Parallel Struggles for a Unified Identity and Symbolization: The Role of Supervision

As Evan has learned how to bring himself more and more into the room and into his relationship with me, I have also had to learn how to bring myself into my new role as his therapist. When I met Evan for the first time, the role of therapist loomed large as a black box of skills and confidence that felt mysterious and elusive. I did not realize that it was not one role I was taking on, but many. I would furthermore learn that the nature of those roles would be defined by Evan and by our relationship, and also by my own readiness to be a bad object, as well as a good one, and to receive Evan's transference reactions.

I was lucky to be told the one thing I most needed to be able to falteringly step into the role of Evan's therapist. In many words, and gestures, and compassionate glances, my supervisor and professors told me that I did not have to know how to be Evan's therapist, and that, in fact, I could not know. My main task was to figure it out, to stay open to possibilities. My supervisor spoke a lot about space, and creating space for Evan to show and tell me things. I found that for me, space was created by focusing carefully on Evan, but that I had to create it for myself as much as for him (Vorus, 2011).

Space and possibilities are hard to come by in the earliest moments of being a therapist. In my first months of being a therapist and working with Evan, the space and time to think before I acted were exactly what felt elusive. While Evan played and I observed, my silences did not feel like a conscious decision, but instead a failure to think fast enough. When I spoke, I never felt sure of what I had said or why, which was terribly disconcerting. My supervisor helped me to turn my focus outward toward Evan, to look at him, hear him, and react to him. I was helped by the idea that it was not that I had to say the perfectly curative thing in the perfect moment, but instead simply see how Evan responded to what I did say. The answer as to whether or not I had done something right was not to be provided by a teacher or professor, but by Evan's response. I could ground myself in observation: by tuning into Evan I would know what effects my words had on him, and I could learn from that about who he was and how to get through to him.

In retrospect, my experience of learning how to be Evan's therapist helped me to understand his experience and inner life. I imagine that Evan has often felt, as I did, as though words and emotions and thoughts were hitting him in the face before he could figure out how to react. His reactions must sometimes feel distressingly out of his control. When initially in the room with Evan, I recognized aspects of his behavior that made me instinctively respond a certain way. In supervision, I struggled to put words to this experience. This is the very definition of lack of space. Words, symbols, and representation create the distance from experience that can feel so vital. The supervisory process put words to my experiences, to my feelings and thoughts and intuitions and worries. In so doing, it gave me some control over the hectic process that is child therapy.

A parallel process was occurring for me in supervision and for Evan in therapy. At first, Evan brought his feelings and experiences into the room in minimally represented forms. His play often seemed to be a direct re-creation of his experience; he lacked the representational ability to play with that experience. His emotions were expressed in the repeated slamming of the elevator door, in his screaming as Kira, and in his throwing tiny plastic child dolls as hard as he could against the far wall of the therapy room. Evan still shows me his feelings as much as he tells me about them, but there is more space to translate them into words and think about them now. We can both see them more clearly for what they are, where they come from, what makes them disappear, what makes them palatable.

An important goal for Evan's treatment is the development of an integrated sense of self, one that he is able to like as well as hate. This requires helping Evan to diminish some of the harsh and punitive tendencies he demonstrates toward himself, in part through allowing him to project them onto me in the transference. This forces me to accept that my role as Evan's therapist involves my being not on' good an' b

or sit quietly with a negative view of one's self, that it requires some coaching. It also requires some distance. As Evan, my supervisor, and I engage in so much parallel process I am careful not to identify with Evan too strongly—by its very nature identification can close the space between us, the space we desperately need to maneuver safely. Similarly, both as my very first patient, and also as a special little guy, Evan is someone I have come to care deeply about. It feels like a new and different way of caring. I am confronted with the task of caring in a way that leaves me open to Evan's experience, for if I am too upset at his sadness or anger I will subtly discourage him from sharing them with me. This necessitates the creation of yet another kind of space, an internal space within which to carry and hold the deep affection I have for Evan, safely and quietly.

Conclusion

More than one year into treatment, Evan is just beginning to openly and directly discuss his past and present with me. More and more, we are becoming real to ourselves and to each other as he develops a more integrated sense of self, and I begin to feel more like a real therapist. Evan is very slowly and simultaneously acquiring the ability to trust me, and to trust himself. It feels as if we have just begun to know each other, to work together, and to create change that can transcend this one special relationship.

References

Fonagy, P., Gergely, G., Jurist, E. L., & Target, M. (2002). *Affect Regulation, Mentalization, and the Development of the Self.* New York: Other Press.

Thompson, A. E. (1986). An object relational theory of affect maturity: Applications to the thematic apperception test. In M. Kissen (Ed.), *Assessing Object Relations Phenomena.* Madison, CT: International Universities Press.

Tuber, S. (2008). *Attachment, Play, and Authenticity: A Winnicott Primer.* Lanham, MD: Jason Aronson.

Tuber, S., & Coates, S. (1985). Interpersonal phenomena in the Rorschachs of extremely feminine boys. *Psychoanalytic Psychology* 2(3), 251–265.

Vorus, N. (2011). Cultivating meaning space: Freudian and neo-Kleinian conceptions of therapeutic action. In A. Druck, C. Ellman, N. Freedman, and A. Thaler (Eds.), *A New Freudian Synthesis: Clinical Process in the Next Generation.* London: Karnac.

3

HOW DO I WORK WITH PARENT *AND* CHILD, ESPECIALLY IF I AM NOT YET A PARENT?

Mougeh Yasai

An Overview

At the start of my second year of graduate school, I was asked to work with my first adolescent patient, D, and her mother, Ms. T. At the time, I felt as though I was entering the murky depths of uncharted waters. I wondered how I would be able to help this mother and her child when I was not yet a mother myself and I was still learning what it takes to be a therapist. I had first been exposed to clinical work only a few months earlier, now I'd been assigned to D's case and I was expected to meet with both Ms. T and D in front of a one-way mirror. Despite my considerable anxiety about the performance aspect of this task, I knew that group supervision would be an invaluable learning experience. Observing other students' first encounter with a parent and a child dyad reminded me that we had similar fears and anxieties, but also some solid training on which we could rely. Over the course of the treatment, I discovered that the support of my colleagues augmented the supervision process in important ways, providing the holding environment that I needed to sustain myself as a beginning therapist.

I was fortunate enough to have a space where I could both seek out and offer support to colleagues, where we could share our hopes and struggles about entering into this new world as developing clinical psychologists. Being a therapist can be a solitary experience and, as someone new to this field, I was filled with the anxiety that came with all that was unknown about this process. In moments of self-doubt, I found refuge by turning to my colleagues who offered different perspectives and a calming reassurance.

The Initial Assessment of the Presenting Problem

Ms. T., a thirty-one year-old Caribbean-American single mother, had first called our clinic after her twelve year-old daughter, D, had written a letter in which she threatened to commit suicide. Ms. T. had a firm and resolute way about her—she seemed in fact at our first meeting, rather formidable, and was clear about her frustration with D and her inability to comprehend D's behavior. But she was also frightened, and knew that both she and her daughter needed help.

In our initial intake, I learned that D had been struggling at school and that her teachers reported that she was inattentive and enmeshed with her peers. The summer prior to our meeting, D had been enrolled in summer school to receive remedial support to help her pass upcoming standardized exams. At that time, D's summer school teachers had contacted the family to report that D had been socializing excessively and had been noncompliant with her schoolwork. According to Ms. T, D's great-grandmother, who was D's other caretaker, had been furious with D and had punished her for her misbehavior. Feeling humiliated, D wrote a suicide note and then ran away from home. In her note, she revealed how she was feeling about herself: "there is no reason to look for me because I am not worth it."

Since then, Ms. T had had further communications from D's teachers, who all reported that D was easily distractible, noncompliant with her schoolwork, and disruptive in class. Ms. T reported that she had tried different things to get her to focus on her schoolwork, such as punishing her by taking privileges away from her, but stated that nothing seemed to help. She had been feeling increasingly frustrated with D for her "headstrong attitude" and her emotional "shutdowns" and was also concerned that D was keeping something from her. Exhausted by D's behavior she felt that she was "at the end of her rope."

Ms. T talked frankly about regretting some of her own life decisions, and concluded that if only she had had a mother who had tended to her more carefully, she would have made better choices in life. She said she feared that D would follow a path similar to her own if she continued to perform poorly in school. Implicitly, she seemed to fear being like her own mother had been, and my sense was that Ms. T did have difficulty attuning to D's needs since she was barely meeting her own needs. Yet, she was insistent that she wanted the very best for D and I could feel that her concerns and fears were genuine. At the same time, I sensed a somewhat natural wish that many parents share, to undo the missteps of their own lives through their children. Ms. T seemed to be translating this into undue pressure on D, combined with an inability to empathize with D's personal struggles and to attune to D's inner life. Exasperated by D, Ms. T noted that it was as though D was a stranger to her, and that she was "at a loss" and unable to handle her.

When I queried Ms. T about any recent noteworthy changes in her family situation, she reported that earlier in the year she had broken up with her long-term partner, who had been living in the home with them. Shortly thereafter, Ms. T had been diagnosed with Rheumatoid Arthritis and she described suffering from a short bout of depression as a consequence. Ms. T stated that D was very helpful and supportive during this time, making dinner for them and keeping track of Ms. T's dietary restrictions. This discussion allowed me to get a sense of Ms. T's vulnerabilities and I was especially struck by her account of her depression. My sense was that she presented herself to the world as a strong, assertive, in control, single mother, but that there was another layer to her personality that she kept hidden from others. I wondered what form her depression had taken and how it had affected D. Was Ms. T harboring resentment for now having to be the sole caretaker for D? Was she worried that Rheumatoid Arthritis would make it hard for her to carry out her responsibilities? Nevertheless, it did seem that when Ms. T was more vulnerable, she actually got along better with D.

Later, after a short time in treatment, I would learn that Ms. T had difficulty shielding D from her inner turmoil and that D was at times overexposed to her mother's moods, much as a sibling or friend might be. I began to wonder how difficult it must be for D to interpret her mother's vacillation from all-knowing and directive, to emotionally chaotic, withdrawn, or angry and somewhat self-involved. This made me think of D's behaviors as acts of reparation (Winnicott, 1965b), and reflect on how much she was dominated my her mother's moods.

Intake Session with D

When I first met D she was starting the 7th grade. I was struck by the contrast between her tall and well-developed physique and her almost childlike facial expressions and mannerisms. D had an overly compliant and cooperative manner. She seemed to want to please me, almost as though this was the only way she knew how to relate to me. But her eagerness to attach lacked the depth in quality that develops over a gradual process of connecting. Along with this false self behavior came a markedly detached quality. She often exhibited blunted affect, making it difficult for me to read her feeling states. In Greenspan and Greenspan's terms (2003), it appeared that D had certain areas of her experience which she had "walled-off." She had become passive and compliant, masking her aggressive and angry feelings in an effort to keep her ill mother close. D's acts of reparation (Winnicott, 1965b) were directed at helping her mother, and so she was left with little understanding of the nature of her own aggression. In turn, she became easily distracted at school, needing to be overly social as a way to ease her depression.

During my initial intake with D, I attempted to gather information about the precipitants to her writing a suicide note. She spoke briefly about her strained relationship with her mother and the difficulty she had focusing on her school-work. D revealed that her mother's diagnosis of Rheumatoid Arthritis was frightening to her and that she witnessed her mother's withdrawal into a depression. She spoke about the pressure to be more independent in response to her mother's illness, for instance, the need to do her own hair since this was now hard for her mother. I noted how she described instances when she either felt overly intruded upon or ignored by her mother. In turn, D responded by withdrawing and self-harming. At first, D reported that she self-sabotaged by being noncompliant with issues related to school, but later in our treatment D revealed more severe self-harming behaviors including self-cutting as a way to soothe herself and to disconnect from her mother.

Formulation From the Initial Assessment

Upon meeting Ms. T, I was immediately aware that we were the same age, and yet we had had vastly different life experiences. She was a mother of a twelve year-old pre-adolescent girl and I was graduate student at the beginning of my training, with little else to worry about other than my own professional development. As the treatment progressed, Ms. T expressed her curiosity about me and would ask me personal questions or would compliment me on my clothing or my jewelry. I experienced these moments as her way of pointing out our differences. She often reflected on her missed educational opportunities and the difficulties that she faced raising a child alone. These interactions with Ms. T left me holding conflicting feelings of sadness, resentment, along with an appreciation of the enormous challenge I faced in helping D and her mother. Until D's treatment, it appeared that Ms. T had no one to turn to for emotional support in her caregiving role. I found myself walking a line between being there for Ms. T while also being mindful of Ms. T's propensity toward blurring boundaries and the effects that this might have on my relationship with D. I was also aware of how her envy of me and my life choices impacted my ability to feel at ease in her presence. In the room with Ms. T, my sense of privilege was unavoidable and there was no escaping it. I wanted to be able to address these issues with her further, but hesitated, as I was unsure whether or not this was deemed appropriate since she wasn't my patient. Looking back on this, I understand my hesitation as a deep fear that this move might disrupt the therapy. On several occasions, I recommended that she seek therapy to help her manage her relationship with D, but she dismissed the idea, stating that she barely had time to keep up with her life now. We revisited the topic regularly but, unfortunately, Ms. T never sought out her own individual treatment. I felt burdened by my desire to undo all that had happened to her in her life, and wondered if D felt that way too. My sense was that Ms. T looked up to me and saw me as someone who had a life of endless possibilities. She would sometimes jokingly make comments about our being the same age and yet having such different lives.

At the end of the assessment, I had some initial thoughts about D's emotional health. I found it somewhat regrettable that Ms. T's career change, which was ostensibly to spend more time and get closer with D, coincided with the onset of D's adolescent desire for independence. It seemed that Ms. T continued to struggle with establishing appropriate mother–daughter boundaries and that this dynamic left D in a constant state of disorganization and confusion. I was struck by Ms. T's keen ability to reflect on the way in which her putting pressure on D to perform better in school was connected to her own fears that D would end up like her, and how this ultimately led to the "shutdowns" that she observed in D. It was difficult to ascertain from the initial assessment whether D's poor performance in school was chronic or whether Ms. T was more aware of it now that she had begun to take a more active role in D's life. Indeed, the moments of connection between mother and daughter still seemed limited because of their busy lives. Ms. T's role as head of the household placed a great strain on her ability to relax and have fun with D. Further, it appeared that Ms. T's relentless focus on improving D's performance at school, while D desired closer and more emotionally connected interactions with her mother, was at the heart of their mis-attunement.

I was left curious about the link between the intermittent role of D's father and her overly social nature. D's deep emotional hunger was largely connected to the disappointment she experienced in her primary relationships, leading to a need to over-socialize as a way to escape her own depression. Her mother's illness further inhibited her ability to express her anger directly and led to the development of an overly and superficially compliant false self.

The Early Stages of Treatment

When I first started to work with D, I struggled to know how best to help her and how to just be in the room with her. One guide was Winnicott's (1971a) notion of the psychotherapeutic task:

> This glimpse of the baby's and child's seeing the self in the mother's face, and afterwards in a mirror, gives a way of looking at analysis and at the psycho-therapeutic task. Psychotherapy is not making clever and apt interpretations; by and large it is a long-term giving the patient back what the patient brings. It is a complex derivative of the face that reflects what is there to be seen.
>
> *(p. 158)*

It took some time for me to realize that what D needed from me most was just that I be there. As a new therapist, I struggled with the pressure I felt from D's mother to come up with quick answers as to why her daughter was shutting down and performing poorly at school. I had to resist both the demands coming from Ms. T and my own desire to demonstrate that I was good at my practice, and instead, patiently make way for D to show me the parts of her that she had felt unsafe to expose. Ms. T would often call and leave me frantic messages, desperate for answers every time D slipped up in school or at home. Although I felt myself being cornered and my boundaries being tested, I made a conscious effort to be there for D's mother. Also I tried to see that the pressure and intrusive quality of Ms. T's interactions with me could provide a window into D's own experience with her mother. In order to provide space for D to open up to me, I felt that I needed to be the holding environment for her mother's anxieties and concerns. I arranged phone sessions with Ms. T when it was difficult for her to come to the clinic and, over time, I started to recognize that by merely reflecting back to her what she gave to me I could be sufficiently comforting and reassuring to her. Still, Ms. T, while at times aware and in touch with her own emotions, was at other times unable to regulate her negative affect.

In my relationship with D, the mere consistency of my presence gradually began to have a stabilizing impact on her. The protection and safety of knowing that I would be there for her two times a week at the same time and in the same place elicited a range of responses from D. On occasion, I would find her waiting for me in the hallway outside of our therapy room, seeming to want to please me. Most of the time, however, she would arrive late, and sometimes toward the very end of our session. Mindful of the way in which many of the people in her life conveyed anger about her misbehavior, I was particularly careful to not be punitive in our exploration about her lateness. This surprised her and she reflected that she couldn't understand why I wasn't more "angry" with her. Over time, we were better able to understand how her lateness was a complex enactment of unprocessed feelings of anger, shame and rejection. This gradually opened up the door to our being able to explore the shame that she often felt about her relationship with her mother, her failures in school and her absent father.

Later on in the treatment, D would be able to reflect on the lack of stability in her life and the way in which our meetings could ground her and give her a sense of safety that she could carry with her to other aspects of her life. In Winnicott's (1965a) terms, my patient had created a false self, likely as the result of some failure in the mirroring process, and her ability to be spontaneous and free were thwarted. D fell within Winnicott's (1965a) third level of false self in which " . . . its main concern (is) a search for conditions which make it possible for the true self to come into its own" (p. 143). The task for me as a therapist was to be good enough to hopefully give her enough space to allow her to be, safely, and on her own. The beginnings of D's coming alive in the therapy only started to unfold after she had built enough faith and trust in me. In likening this process to the one that occurs between mother and infant, Tuber (2008) states that:

> what comes out of being able to use an object is that the baby has faith in that object. The baby comes to trust that that object is going to be there and that is where the very notion of faith comes from.
>
> *(Tuber, 2008, p. 87)*

It is worth noting at this point that early on in the treatment, I had recommended that D have a psycho-diagnostic assessment to help clarify her cognitive and psychological functioning. Ms. T had D tested at her school and the results of the testing indicated average intelligence. After reviewing her test results, I felt reassured to find that D's poor school performance had more to do with socio-emotional forces rather than a pure cognitive limitation. My sense was that D was an inquisitive young girl and that her lack of motivation and disinterest at school were connected to the issues she was having at home. The results of her TAT and Rorschach, provided by a research-based psychological assessment at our clinic, revealed that D could be impulsive and could lose reality testing when confronted with strong affect. The results further indicated that D was attempting to contain a frightening inner life, filled with menacing internal representations, but lacked the resources to self-soothe. The themes of her responses were dominated by anger, sadness and unpredictability. She was quick to disavow her aggressive impulses that were lying just below the surface.

In addition to confirming some of my own early clinical observations, the results of the psychological assessment pointed me to her tendency to lose reality testing when faced with intensely charged affects. Indeed, later in the treatment, the issue of her reality testing came up with my clinic director and my supervisor, and it was this knowledge in conjunction with my own observations that helped me make a more thoughtful recommendation for her continued treatment.

Some Early Sessions with D

In the beginning of the treatment, I struggled to make sense of my feelings for D. On the one hand, it felt satisfying to have my adolescent patient like me, but on the other hand I was puzzled and saddened by her disconnected affect. Why did I feel so much emptiness in the room with her? Indeed, her quick relatedness left me with an unsettled feeling. It reminded me of Greenspan's (2003) description of emotional promiscuity in children being a possible indicator of an early history of deprivation. I began to wonder about how this put D at risk when relating with others, both her peers and adults.

Play

From the beginning of our treatment, it became apparent that D was less comfortable with "talk therapy" and was more interested in the games and toys in the child therapy room. It was not until much later in the treatment when we had transitioned out of the child therapy room into an adult therapy room, that she was able to talk more explicitly about her feelings of anger, shame and sadness.

"Sorry," D sheepishly said after winning our game of Sorry. "I didn't mean to kill you!" Through our play sessions, I learned that while D wanted to please me, she could also be aggressive and distancing. She really did want to "kill me" at Sorry, but was afraid that I would be unable to accept those feelings, and would become angry and retaliate. For many months, D and I would play Sorry and other similar board games. The themes that emerged in our play were that of surviving loss, and managing competitive and aggressive feelings. D struggled with asserting herself in our play, and would repeatedly have an apologetic tone and look on her face when she would win. Overly concerned about my reaction to her every move, she would shy away from expressing her aggressive and competitive urges. This left me grappling with my feelings of frustration and boredom in the therapy. Sharing these issues with my supervisor and fellow classmates, I began to have a deeper understanding of the notion of countertransference. D's projected feelings of boredom were a defense against the intolerable feelings of anger and sadness that led to her emotional shutdowns and her disconnected affect. Unsure of how to proceed and aware of how much space her mother took up in her life, I too was overly concerned about how she might experience me. With time, I understood that D could tolerate my increasing presence in the room, and in turn, I became more comfortable naming the complex feelings that came up around competition in our play.

A parallel process seemed to be occurring with my supervisor. Like D, I felt myself shrinking away and becoming overly compliant in an effort to win him over. This was my very first adolescent patient, and although I had worked with adolescents in a teaching capacity, I didn't yet feel confident in my clinical skills. My supervisor's response to the parallel process allowed me to see an area of impasse in my treatment with D. It was not through empty praise of my work but rather through his constant frank approach that I was able to recognize my developing skills as a clinician. After watching me handle a crisis situation with D and her family, he shared his honest appreciation of my work.

I began to see how D's shrinking away from being real in the room, and my continuing to smooth things over, were limiting her from engaging in any real relationship with me. When she engaged in cutting behavior, I notified her mother of the incident, and with the consultation of the clinic staff, it was recommended that she be evaluated at the nearest psychiatric Emergency Room (ER). My supervisor, who was unreachable at the time of the crisis, was in disagreement with the clinic staff's decision to send her to the ER. This created tension between them, and left me in the awkward position of needing to answer to both parties while also keeping my patient in the forefront of the discussion. Despite his reservations about the decision to send D to the ER, my supervisor acknowledged that I was able to hold onto my own clinical judgment while balancing the clinic's recommendation. Prior to this incident, D and I had discussed her urge to self-harm and I had made it clear that it would be important for me inform her mother if I became aware of this behavior. When D came to our session with cuts along her arm, I conveyed my concern for D's emotional health while also remaining firm in regard to her physical well-being. In the moment, I was worried that she experienced my informing her mother as a betrayal. The intervention, however, had a stabilizing effect on her and, in fact, it was my taking her situation seriously that allowed her to build a stronger trust and faith in me. Indeed, this was a new way of relating for D. Typically, D was either ignored or responded to with a negative intensity that was not accompanied by a thoughtful explanation nor by a consideration for her mind. D began to recognize that I was genuinely interested in her internal experience, and in turn, she became better able to expose her anger and sadness authentically.

One Session: D's Divided Heart

In one of our sessions during the first year of treatment, D drew a picture of a heart split into two pieces with hate on one side and love on the other. In this session, D begins to show me her struggle with integrating these charged emotions. Below is an excerpt from this session.

(D is drawing a heart meticulously she puts a line through the middle and writes hate and love on either side of the heart.)

D: Not done yet . . . a lot more to it . . . . . a whole lot more. It is going to look really nice. Happy on this side. (D is drawing with focus. This takes quite a while to do.)

T: I can see that . . . lots of concentration. It is important to get it just right, huh?

D: Uh huh. I drew this once in art and I forgot to draw rain and that is the biggest part of this side.

D meticulously illustrates the way in which she views love and hate as two separate and distinct feelings as they relate to her object world. D's detailed approach and persistence in getting it "just right" is her way to manage the intense feelings that come up for her during this session. I respond by attempting to affirm her desire to make sense of this internal struggle.

T: It looks like there is a lot more hate in the heart than love.

D: It is going to be the same thing. The same thing on the other side too. May I see red?

Here, I jump in too quickly and D backs away in an effort to hold onto the idea of these feelings being separate and equal.

T: Yes, you may.

D: You want black?

T: Sure

D: The heart is split, which is why I put the line down the middle. Dead grass is like brown, right?

T: Yeah . . . brown, beige, yellow. Brown sounds good. (D continues to work on the heart) Love and hate are feelings that sometimes touch each other, huh?

D: Uh huh. (Continues to work almost as if I am not there and talks to herself) Do I need more red? Yes, I do.

The image of the heart split down the middle reflects her difficulty in integrating part-objects. For D, love and hate have clear boundaries and she struggles with being able to hold both of these feelings together at the same time. My noting that these two parts are touching is an attempt to allow her to recognize that loving and hateful feelings can coexist.

T: There are a lot of flowers growing on the love feeling side.
D: Uh huh.
T: The sky is clear on the love feeling side . . .
D: I have to do this side first because this (pointing to the hate feeling side) needs more time
T: A little more complicated?
D: (She nods) Isn't this side pretty?
T: It is pretty.

D is beginning to acknowledge the difficulty in addressing her sad and angry feelings, but has a hard time holding onto them for long, and shifts to the "pretty" loving feelings. I, too, struggle with allowing her space to feel uncomfortable and respond by praising her work.

D: I need the black for one more thing
T: Of course. The black is yours.
D: No more bright colors. I only need . . . (She's picking through dark colors to color her hate side)
T: Any of these dark colors work?
D: I need brown . . . red . . . all of these colors . . . these are the colors I need for this side. (Drawing on the hate side) Those are rain clouds . . . it is not supposed to look very pretty.

D has a child-like understanding of love and hate as being equated to pretty and ugly. D uses a primary defensive process of splitting and has a hard time making sense of ambivalence. She needs to organize her world by keeping images of good and bad separate and isolated from one another.

T: The flowers are dying on the hate side.
D: Uh huh (she is drawing more vigorously).
T: The hate feelings are making the flowers die, huh?
D: Uh huh.
T: And that flower even lost some of its yellow, some of its bright color.
D: The other part . . . this whole thing.

T: Is it raining or storming?
D: Raining
T: Rain feelings are like a release.

Here, I am attempting to expand and articulate her internal experience. At times, however, I rush in to ease her tension by offering her a reassuring comment rather than allowing her to sit and work through her discomfort.

D: It's better with a pencil though, because you can see all the details. There can't be a gap (she's referring to the rain drops), it can't be like that . . .
T: It kind of covers you, the rain. (D meticulously draws rain drops.) We have around 5 minutes left.
D: Ok, coming.
T: A lot of rain!
D: Uh huh.
T: The hate feelings are raining.
D: What a lot of work to do!
T: Hard work!
D: Uh huh, it hurts your hands. Almost done.
T: Wow!
D: That was fast, huh?
T: Sometimes the hate feelings and the love feelings feel like two separate pieces of us.
D: They do, they really do.
T: They really do.
D: Phew!
T: Wow!
D: Do you like it?
T: I do. I like it a lot.
D: Which side do you think looks the best?
T: I think you can have a little bit of both, D. (She smiles) So I like them both.

D, struggling with integrating these feelings, turns to me to ask me which one I like best. In an effort to allow her to see that both can exist at the same, I state that I like them both. Although I am trying to convey an ability to hold both feeling states, I don't speak to the internal struggle that goes on when attempting to make sense of these strong feelings.

Another Session: D's Toy Animals

The excerpt from the following session reveals D's progress in treatment over a year later. In this session, D reveals the deep feelings of sadness and anger that she holds toward her mother for forcing her to give away her toy animals. D's transitional objects (Winnicott, 1971b) have been forcibly taken from her and she reflects on her own struggle living in this in-between state.

T: Was your giant purple elephant the one that sleeps next to you?
D: Not anymore. That's the one my Mom made me give away. I am so mad! Violet.
T: Violet. Violet is gone.
D: (She nods) She made me give away all my teddy bears. I was so not even mad . . . I was livid.
T: Mad. Livid.

Here, D is openly talking about how deprived she feels and how angry she is at her mother. I begin by reflecting back her experience in an effort to stay closely attuned.

D: I was livid and distraught. So mad!
T: So many feelings around losing those teddy bears. Those teddy bears used to live on your bed? In your room?
D: (She nods)
T: They would sleep next to you. You would cuddle next to Violet.
D: Violet was too big to sleep in my bed but sometimes. I won her at Six Flags. Ring toss. I did the ring toss and I won her. And I loved her even though her throat kept opening and I kept giving her surgery.
T: So Violet has been through a lot with you. You won her, and you took care of her, and you sewed her up?

D is using grown-up words to describe her deep feelings about this loss of a part of her childhood. D's description of her lost animals reflects her longing to hold onto her younger self and yet the need to be more "adult" is shown through her word choice. I attempt to expand her experience by speaking to the many complex feelings that come up with this abrupt deprivation. It would have been helpful to speak more explicitly about these feelings and about being between childhood and adolescence.

D: And then I had Cream . . . Creamy. This big bear. I went to Six Flags for this trip. My mom gave me like fifty dollars and it was like forty something dollars, and I only needed like two quarters left and I really wanted that bear so I walked around all of Six Flags to find two quarters on the floor because I really wanted that bear.
T: Wow, a lot of dedication there. You found the two quarters.
D: I gave the guy the money and I was like I will be right back and I was sure to get that bear.
T: That was Creamy.

D: The last night I had her I changed her to a him.

T: The last night you had her was the last night before you gave away all of your teddy bears?

D: Uh huh.

T: What was the change for?

D: I don't know. I felt like making it a boy . . . Kareem because he is like my brother on my father's side and I had a crush on him for a long time, but I think I am finally over him, but I just wanted to name him Kareem. And I always called Kareem whipped cream anyways because his name is K-a-r-e-e-m. His Mom Kim said I said why did you name your son Kareem? Because when he was born he looked like cream, so his name is Kareem.

T: And Cream was first a girl and then a boy?

D speaks about her great efforts at winning this bear and how the only power she had, at the very last moment, was to change the bear from a her to a him. I now understand this as her need to unconsciously split off the internalized rejecting object (mother) from the internalized loving object. In the moment, I am thrown off and instead ask her why she made the change. Unable to answer the question, D breaks from the material and begins to fill the space with unrelated details.

D: Creamy.

T: Creamy.

D: Because she had creamy fur. It was really light brown.

T: Did you know Creamy would go away the next day?

D: It wasn't the next day, it was a while afterward when me and my Mom had an argument.

T: I remember that.

D: I don't think I will ever forgive her for all my teddy bears.

T: Yeah it must feel hard to forgive that.

D articulates the anger she feels toward her mother and acknowledges that she will continue to hold onto this painful memory.

D: If she asked me what I wanted for Christmas, I would say I want all my teddy bears back. I want to see what she says.

T: It's a big wish to get them all back

D: I've had some of them since I was a baby.

T: So it's not just teddy bears in some store. They have lots of meaning for you. You want those teddy bears back . . . , some you got when you were a baby, some when you were older.

D: My dad wants me to think about it as giving it to a child who don't have any toys. But they probably do. I was so hurt when I saw this Spanish lady take Kareem. I was speaking to the lady who took Violet. I was so mad.

T: Painful, angry. You must have felt very angry.
D: Uh huh. I still think about them. I look in my room. I keep thinking because my mom cleaned my room. When I look at it I think where would Violet be sitting right now?
T: They are still part of you. You still keep them in your mind.

D speaks of the hope she has to be nurtured. She regresses and her voice takes on a younger child-like tone, almost as though she were speaking as her younger child-like self. D speaks again of her feelings of deprivation and anger at being pushed out of her childhood. I felt closely connected to D during this session and, although intermittently, her real self began to surface. In this session, she begins to show a capacity to elaborate and begin to process her painful feelings.

In the early phase of the treatment, D was working through the feelings that she had around being pushed into a more adult role. This struggle came out in her initial desire to play and to engage with me on a more child-like level. After being able to show me her younger child self, she gradually began to acknowledge the part of her that was sad for this abrupt loss, and was slowly able to acknowledge a desire to enter adolescence. This shift is a difficult one for girls in particular, and I resonated with her loss of her little girl self.

Progress in D's Treatment

About halfway through our treatment, D made the decision that she was ready to move to an adult therapy room. We had stopped playing board games for some time and instead spent the sessions talking. She reflected on how much she had changed from the start of our treatment, how "young" she once was and how ready she felt to transition to an adult therapy room. This was a watershed moment in the treatment. I felt as though D had come a long way. When I had met her, she was barely able to name her feelings or to connect her behavior to her feelings and now she was beginning to come alive. Not surprisingly, my bored feelings gradually began to dissipate and I was beginning to feel a more genuine sense of connectedness between us. She reflected on how the adult therapy room had once scared her because she feared being required to talk the whole time. She laughed, saying that now she wasn't afraid of talking to me.

As D's therapy continued, she gained increasing insight into her dissociated feelings. She began to see how she used behaviors like self-cutting to cope with anger which needed to be articulated and processed. On multiple occasions, D's mother had read her diary, discovering D's angry feelings toward her. This stirred up a great deal of anxiety for Ms. T who felt threatened and uncertain about D's emotional state. I worked with Ms. T to allow D to have space and reassured her that D needed to have a place to express her frustrations. Having acknowledged that cutting was her way of releasing pent-up anger toward her mother,

D needed help with expressing her anger more constructively. To that end, we created a "feeling box," a private space where she could record, reflect upon and store her feelings. At first she stared blankly at the paper and the box, but after some time she genuinely appreciated being able to have this private space.

D noted a recurrent enactment with her mother in which she responded to her mother's volatile moods and blow-ups by dissociating and then later releasing her anger against herself either by cutting or getting into trouble with her mother about school. She recognized that this dynamic imbued her with a feeling of being defeated and helpless, and that this reaction is self-harming. With both D and Ms. T, we explored ways in which D could alert her mother whenever she experienced angry and self-harming feelings; Ms. T could then better control her own angry reactions. The intervention felt most useful in initiating a dialogue about their underlying dynamic: D's withdrawal and self-harming behavior and Ms. T's explosive anger and intrusiveness. Ms. T later reported to me in our phone sessions that she was now more aware of her tendency to lose control and to overreact.

One of the ongoing issues in the treatment was that while D was overly preoccupied with pleasing me, these placating behaviors also had an aggressive component that served to keep me at arm's length. While providing D with some sense of emotional control, placating and distancing also increased her loneliness and depression. As the treatment progressed, I became more able to tolerate my own discomfort with this behavior. This in turn, allowed her to show me her feelings of loneliness, depression and vulnerability. Rather then rushing to support her and to make her "feel better" during moments of anxiety or sadness, I challenged myself to sit back and observe how she handled being overwhelmed and allowed the session to unfold. This was a developmental shift for me, since I felt maternal toward her and I found myself naturally wanting to smooth things over and to minimize conflict and anxiety. By being allowed space to sit with these uncomfortable feelings, D gradually began to develop enough trust in me to allow these moments of vulnerability to occur without an immediate shutdown. As a result, she was able to experience an increasing range of feeling, as well as greater intimacy with me. D continued to struggle with connecting meaning to her behavior, but began to gradually express frustration and slowly identify connections between her feelings and her behavior.

Like most adolescents, D grew increasingly preoccupied with her peers and developed a heightened interest in the opposite sex. She often turned to her social world as an escape from facing her difficulties at school and at home. She would frequently shift the conversation in our sessions to issues related to her peers and boys, particularly when she was avoiding a more distressing topic. Once we identified this pattern, she began to gain an awareness of her tendency to switch topics as a way to fend off her negative feelings.

Overall, D's general functioning had improved since the start of treatment, albeit, at the time of termination, she was continuing to experience inconsistent performance at school. Toward the end of our treatment, D progressed in her ability to address issues of concern about her living situation, conflicts with her mother and struggles with school. Further, she was better able to tolerate the anxiety and depression associated with the dissatisfactions and frustrations of her life.

Termination

At this early point in my professional life, my understanding was that most therapies arrive at termination when therapist and patient mutually agree that the patient's initial presenting problem has been ameliorated and/or intrapsychic change had been achieved, and when there has been some form of resolution of feelings through the transference. My treatment with D, however, ended because I was moving on to another stage in my professional development. After much discussion about the course of the treatment and D's current mental health status, it was decided that D could benefit from further treatment and that she should be transferred to another student clinician in our clinic. Despite my knowing about this end point from the onset, the termination still felt abrupt and unsettling. After several years of treating D, I had come to feel responsible for her and her mother. I was left with a sense that our socio-economic difference was once again revealing itself as problematic in this final phase of the treatment. I was the graduate student whose years of training and opportunity were now allowing her to move on. I was the one who had taken D and her mother down this long path, only to suddenly let go just when the treatment had finally started to have a positive effect. I wondered if D and her mother would understand how disappointed I was to be unable to "see things through," and how important they, my very first child therapy clients, would always remain to me. After all, she would always be my very first child therapy case and this case would forever live on in me.

I did feel glad that a discussion about the termination had been a part of the treatment from the very beginning. I had been mindful to be open with D and her mother about my being a trainee and about the time, in the foreseeable future, when our treatment would have come to an end. Over time, D was able to be explicit about her attachment to me and to the clinic, and she would often speak about her reluctance to accept the inevitable termination. Although she would characteristically articulate her sad and disappointed feelings, she had a harder time expressing her anger toward me. Because anger was generally acted out and dissociated for D, the months leading up to the termination began to feel very much like the beginning of our treatment. D would often spend most of a session filling our time with a series of stories about her social life. Again, I would leave our sessions with an empty feeling, though not quite bored as in our early sessions. Sometimes D would skip our session altogether and would leave me a message stating the reason for her "no show." The following session usually started with an apology for missing our session. We would spend some time exploring her absences and her need to apologize for them. It was difficult for D to hate me. She couldn't tolerate it. There was so much disappointment in her life that she couldn't let that happen. It took some time for D to link these disconnected feelings with the deep sense of disappointment she had experienced in her relationship with her father. She began to talk about how often she had waited for him only to have him not show up. It was becoming clear how hard it was for her to open herself up to any form of real connectedness, like a desire for closeness or a feeling of hate and anger.

After some discussion, my supervisor and I decided that given the absence of male figures in D's life, she might benefit from working with a male therapist. I had felt for some time that D's burgeoning sexuality was bringing up issues with men, and that a male therapist might give her an opportunity to work through some of those issues. I knew that so many of D's relationships were unstable, and that she had looked at our relationship as one of the few constants in her life. It seemed particularly important that she not experience the transfer as a casual and thoughtless process. My intention was to include D in our discussion about the transfer, allowing her to feel like she was an active participant in the therapeutic process and in the change of therapists. I also hoped that D would be able to address her angry feelings toward me, so that they would not get acted out after the transfer and sabotage her work with her new therapist.

In my supervision sessions, I processed my own guilt feelings and my uncertainty about passing along the treatment to a less experienced therapist. I wondered how far D would regress during the transition and whether she would be able to make a real connection with her new clinician. Fears of my own incompetence began to surface as I worried about not having helped her enough and about having somehow missed something in the treatment that would be discovered by D's new therapist. But I was comforted by the thought that, however things turned out between D and her new therapist, she would now have a new relationship, another positive internalized other to hold onto and carry with her.

In our final session, D and Ms. T shared their appreciation for my always being there to "weather the storm" with them. The sentiment was mutual. I knew that the path to becoming a therapist would not be a straight or easy one. It would take time and experience for me to come to an understanding of the subtleties that occur in the change process. I carried on with the belief that with more experience, I would begin to feel more certain that I could have a lasting and positive effect on my patients. However, I was aware that part of this was my own process, my way of finding a space for myself to exist as a therapist, somewhere between an imagined ideal and the reality of self-doubt that came along with my being new to this field. My hope was that Ms. T and D would continue to live their lives changed in some way by our encounter. And I have no doubt that I also have been changed and that I am a more effective therapist now than I was when I first met D and her mother.

References

Greenspan, S. & Greenspan, N. T. (2003). *The Clinical Interview of the Child*. Washington DC: American Psychiatric, Inc.

Tuber, S. (2008). *Attachment, Play, and Authenticity: A Winnicott Primer*. Lanham, MD: Jason Aronson.

Winnicott, D.W. (1965a). Ego distortion in terms of true and false self. In D. W. Winnicott, *The Maturational Processes and the Facilitating Environment*. New York: International Universities Press.

Winnicott, D. W. (1965b). Reparation in respect of a mother's organized defence against depression. In D. W. Winnicott, *Playing and Reality*. London: Tavistock Publications.

Winnicott, D. W. (1971a). Mirror-role of mother and family in child development. In D. W. Winnicott, *Playing and Reality*. London: Tavistock Publications.

Winnicott, D. W. (1971b). Transitional objects and transitional phenomena. In D. W. Winnicott, *Playing and Reality*. London: Tavistock Publications.

4

HOW DO I WORK LONG-TERM WITH A CHILD WHEN I ONLY HAVE A YEAR TO WORK WITH HIM?

The Conflicts Inherent in Time-Limited Therapy while in Clinical Training

Elizabeth Freidin Baumann

William was referred to me at the beginning of my year-long clinical psychology internship at a hospital-based outpatient clinic. When I first met this eight-year-old boy, I quickly fell in love with his sharp intellect, inquisitive nature, creative thinking and high verbal capacity. He was a beautiful child who was ready to connect and show me the world through his eyes. He was originally referred to psychotherapy by his psychiatrist for symptoms that included a need for control over his environment, difficulty shifting activities and hyperactivity. In the evaluation process it became evident that William's behavioral difficulties were causing relational problems with his adoptive parents at home.

Conversations with his adoptive parents gave a context for William's symptoms. They revealed that William had been neglected by his biological mother in the first year of life and subsequently adopted out of foster care. They also talked about how, while they were extremely committed to raising him, his hyperactivity, anxiety and need for control at home was taking a toll. It was powerful for them to discuss how William's life was so vastly different from how it could have turned out, and how even after adoption William continued to carry with him a history of early neglect.

The Fantasy Animal Drawing: EagleLion

Though he was an inquisitive child and eager to connect, early sessions with William felt rigid and defended, similar to his reported behavior at home. He would begin each session with a list of games we should play, mostly of a competitive nature, and would stiffen if I suggested or made a motion toward a change in routine. While these first sessions left me frustrated at his inability to play, they provided me with a vivid understanding of how the capacity for play (Winnicott, 1969) did not yet feel safe enough for William. His interaction with the games indicated themes of aggression and need for control. However, when I commented on the aggression, he seemed unable to reflect and would quickly switch the activity.

Instead of letting this rigid pattern unfold on its own time, knowing that we had less than a year of weekly treatment to work with, I thought it might be helpful in this beginning phase of the work to "test the limits" of William's capacity for play. I was curious about the edges of William's fantasy life and how much displacement could be used in this treatment to access the themes of early maternal loss. I suggested to William that we create a Fantasy Animal Drawing (Handler & Hilsenroth, 1994).

William seemed to love the structure of a "task" that he had to accomplish (given that free play was too anxiety-provoking at this point). Preferring to write a story instead of drawing a picture (since this was not a formal projective assessment but rather a rapport-building exercise, I did not insist), William immediately took to this task. The following is William's verbatim description of his Fantasy Animal, the "EagleLion":

> The EagleLion lives on the ground and in the trees because it can fly. The EagleLion is a child that became lost from his parents because he flew off because when his mother turned her back. He said "I want to sneak off and fly off" but then he got lost without his mother knowing. He's thinking: "I'm all alone and no one followed me and now I'm really scared. I should go home instead of being lost because it's kind of getting dark out here. And I'm really lost now that it's dark in the sky! If I land out of the nest I can get eaten. What else can I try to do? Oh maybe I can be camouflaged. No one will notice if I change my own color. Before I can think about landing, I'm hungry. Now that I ate I should go back to the nest by the time it's morning. Mother must be worried about me."

I was astounded as this story poured out of William and onto the page like it had been patiently waiting its turn to be written. As I recounted the session in supervision the next week, we discussed how the themes of the treatment had unfolded right in front of us. William had been waiting to tell us his story: he just needed an opening to be heard. In our thematic analysis of his Fantasy Animal story, my supervisor observed that William felt the need to turn passive into active in order to make sense of his mother's abandonment. We talked about how the EagleLion was William's attempt at regaining control over what he had lost so early in his life. In William's story, he had created a situation in which he had only himself to blame, clearly as a way to make sense of his mother's abandonment. The EagleLion story was William's way of telling me that he was still lost, hungry and in search of his mother.

The EagleLion as Transitional Object

Once the EagleLion was created, he never left our relationship. Indeed, after this initial exercise, as William and I continued to build a special world inside the walls of our treatment room, the EagleLion quickly became our imaginary friend, his story deepening and developing in line with the treatment. Over the next few months, the EagleLion developed into our transitional object (Winnicott, 1971a), a co-created object that could witness and represent William's experience in treatment. Soon, William began almost every session by going to the computer in the room and pretending to receive an email from EagleLion, often with urgent information about his whereabouts and safety. Via these 'emails,' William invited the EagleLion into our space, into our developing narrative. William would also bring the EagleLion himself into our sessions, by suddenly getting quiet, pausing and whispering, "I think he's here with us now." "What's he saying now?" I would gingerly inquire.

Themes of Maternal Loss

Using EagleLion as a gateway, William found a portal through which to move towards exploration of deeper themes of rage, abandonment and loss. During each treatment session, I hoped that we would encounter EagleLion and simultaneously feared what would happen if we did. One day, William "received" a particularly upsetting email from EagleLion. "You're not going to want to hear what the EagleLion told me," William said with fear in his eyes. "What is it?" I inquired, nervous to hear the response.

P: The EagleLion is in trouble because he killed his family.
T: What? Why did he kill his family?
P: He didn't mean to. Actually an evil spirit possessed him and made him do it. He didn't mean to do it. He feels really bad and mad at the person who made him do it.
T: Oh, poor EagleLion, he must be so sad now that he lost his family. What is he going to do?
P: He doesn't know. He has us though. We are his friends.

Until this moment, I did not know how actively William had been processing our work regarding displacement in early infancy and the loss of his mother. His adoptive parents had told me that his biological mother had other children who were also removed from her custody. They told me that they did not know who William's father was. Through the EagleLion, William told me that he was struggling with these unknowns with this unspoken narrative that he was just beginning to symbolize.

Through the EagleLion, William was able to access an unconscious belief that he felt responsible for the loss of his mother. He was able to use the displacement to tap into his aggression and his fear that he may have accidentally killed off his family. His neglect during early childhood seemed to inhibit William and made it too scary for him to think about his mother's thoughts about him, as these thoughts would lead to the idea that she left him, and perhaps a wish to actually harm him. Just as the EagleLion is lost in the woods, so too William feels that his mother left him lost, hungry and alone.

As we entered the winter of our year-long work together, sessions during which EagleLion would be in desperate need of help were common. In supervision, I discussed how William needed to show me how out of control he felt around this destructive, aggressive part of himself, the part that in his mind, abandoned his mother. We let the EagleLion come and go as needed. William would tell me when he was visiting or sending us an email, but his presence was intense and fleeting. No matter how much trouble he was in, there was nothing we could do to help him.

One day, William came into a session worried that we would be disturbed by the other children in the clinic.

P: I have an idea! Let's put a "Do Not Disturb" sign on our door. I hear kids in the hallway. I don't want them to come in. (William makes a sign and asks for tape. We adhere it to the front of our door.)

T: Now it's just us.

P: Wait, I think the EagleLion is emailing us. Let me check. (William goes to the computer and pretends to type furiously.) The EagleLion has one message for us. He needs our help because his city is burning down. He has no home. He needs water. He needs food.

T: Oh no! It sounds like the EagleLion is in a lot of trouble. I'm so glad he emailed you. What are we going to do?

P: (William begins to type furiously again.) It's sad. Very sad. He actually says there is nothing we can do. Just hope that he will be ok. That we should just think about him. No one can help him now.

T: Sounds like EagleLion is on his own right now. I'm feeling like he needs us but we can't help him.

P: What will people think when they see the sign on our door?

T: What do you think?

P: That we are glad to see each other. Do you see other kids? I know you must because if you didn't, it would be like you were family.

T: It feels like I am in your family. You wish that I were family?

P: Yeah, like you are an aunt.

T: It feels like we are that close. What would be good about me being in your family?

P: Then I could see you every day.

T: That would feel nice, right?

P: Yeah.

Conversations like this were painful for me to bear. I perceived how strongly connected to me William felt, and how scary it was for him to experience the fear of loss. As the months went on and William, EagleLion and I continued to build a relationship in the treatment room, I began to worry about how the working through of maternal loss was going to be intensified by termination at the end of my training year.

Termination: The EagleLion and Working Through

Indeed, though his role in the middle phase of the treatment was to help William process the loss of his mother, the EagleLion played a different yet equally power-ful role in the months leading up to our much-anticipated termination. Though William's parents had known from the outset that the treatment was only a year long due to the constraints of my training position, the impact of the termination hit the family hard. For William, whose mother left him without reason or expla-nation in the first months of life, the termination brought up previously untapped feelings of abandonment. Indeed, though painful, the termination and working through of this goodbye were in essence a powerful tool to bring themes of loss and mourning into the play.

   With a pending termination in late June, I began to prepare William to say goodbye starting in early May. William wanted to know how long it would be until he could see me again. He made a chart showing weeks, months and years. When I had to tell him that we might not ever be able to see each other again, he could not hear that and emphatically stated, "Two years." It was excruciat-ing for me to tell him that it might not be two years; it might be never. As the pending goodbye sunk in, EagleLion became the outlet for William's mounting anger toward me for abandoning him. William, the boy, was left innocent and connected so that I could continue to care for him. Using EagleLion, we were able to express our outrage at the arbitrary parameters of the termination.

P: Sorry to break the news, but the EagleLion says he has to go.
T: Really? We didn't even get a chance to say goodbye.
P: (William pretends to listen to what the EagleLion is whispering to him) What? For that long? You've got to be kidding me, EagleLion. You're not going to be back for two years?
T: Oh, EagleLion, that's a long time. We are really going to miss you.
P: Come on, EagleLion, that is such a long time. It feels like a long time. It feels like a century.
T: Oh, come on, EagleLion, it's so painful.
P: Yeah, come on, EagleLion.
T: We are going to miss you so much!
P: We will be so lonesome without you. Come on, EagleLion, don't you think you could just stay for a while?

T: It is so hard to say goodbye to our friend.

P: And it will be hard to say goodbye to you. We will really miss each other for a long time.

T: We really will miss each other. We are going to think about each other. And it is so hard when someone goes away without you wanting them to.

P: It is so hard. It is impossible to think of.

The pain I felt after William left this session was immense. In supervision, there was space for me to acknowledge that I was holding William's history of feeling left and abandoned not just by me but also by his mother. My supervisor helped me see that this goodbye would not be as easy as it seemed. Underneath our proper goodbyes to each other and EagleLion, my supervisor warned that I might be missing that William was angry with me for leaving. By "making" the EagleLion leave before we had to say goodbye, he was taking away our connection before I had the chance to. I knew that this interpretation of what William did with EagleLion was true, but it was hard to accept. I felt incredible guilt that William had to do this. For a child who was abandoned so early in his life, and who was trusting enough to use the treatment as a means to work through these feelings, I felt the cruelty of our pending termination. On the other hand, I used supervision to discuss how, because the treatment opened up in the way that it did, William felt abandoned by me, precisely because he was left before. Intellectually, I knew that it showed great strength in this eight-year-old boy to feel safe enough to explore these feelings of abandonment in displacement. But still, as the one who was holding them, the pain was excruciating.

Our discussions of goodbyes did not last a long time. The EagleLion could not just leave and go to a safe place, not when he was coming from William's fantasies. Going back to the original Fantasy Animal story, we know that the EagleLion did not just leave the nest able to find his way in the world. He was scared, hungry and in danger. And that is exactly where we began our next session: in danger.

In our next session, William came into the room and quickly informed me that we had received an 'email' from the EagleLion with some distressing news. The email informed him that EagleLion had been out in the woods searching for food and was killed by a hunter. Here was the anger that my supervisor and I had predicted. William had clearly absorbed during our last session that our pending termination was inevitable. No matter how much pain he expressed to me, I had not been able to change the outcome of the termination. His solution, therefore, was to kill off not only the part of himself that was "searching for food," but also the part of himself that had a special connection to me. It was an expression of his anger at me and his way of processing the reality of our termination.

My countertransference surrounding EagleLion's death was immediate and devastating. As we made a funeral pyre out of paper in the middle of the room and said our goodbyes to our friend, I felt that I had let William down. I wanted to mourn EagleLion's death together as a way to mourn the loss of our relationship. "Let's remember the good times we had with the EagleLion," I said to William. What I struggled with was that my sadness at EagleLion's death eclipsed my ability to see the aggression in William's act of killing off our special friend.

The Role of Supervision in the Termination Process

The death of EagleLion in our sessions hit me hard. I felt responsible for offering William a promise of my love and care, and incredibly guilty that I had to terminate with him due to the end of my training at the clinic. I was pulled to talk with William about our positive experiences with EagleLion while forgoing his expression of aggression in the act of killing our friend. The pain and guilt that I was holding in transference was not only mine, but was also his mother's who left him. I was at first unable to see the anger and the aggression in William's destruction of our creation, the EagleLion.

My supervision helped me to recognize how hard I was working to avoid the anger towards me. Conversations in supervision also helped me to acknowledge William's own need for destruction. To kill off the EagleLion was William's attempt to kill off that part of himself that felt alone, vulnerable and abandoned. To kill off the EagleLion was also to sever our connection. With this he aimed to sever the connection that felt safe enough to have with me in the treatment. William was furious that it was ending just at a point where he began to feel our bond.

The EagleLion Goes Home

Possibly as his way to protect me from my own feelings of sadness around the end of our relationship, or his own feelings of discomfort with his own aggression, William could not keep the EagleLion dead for long. The next session, William came into the room and informed me that the EagleLion had come back as an angel.

P: He came back as an angel maybe to protect me. Guard you so you will not be hurt.
T: I can't believe that he is not dead!
P: I know. But he is in danger.
T: Oh, wow. What are we going to do?
P: I don't know.
T: What's life like for him now?
P: Scary. Because now that he is alive the EagleLion newspaper says, "Dead EagleLion returns."

T: Sounds like he needs protection.
P: Maybe he should go home with me.
T: That's a great idea. Did you ask him if he wanted to?
P: He said yeah. He said I have the right foods that he likes.
T: Sounds like you can really take care of him. And maybe he can take care of you.

At the end of that session, William "put" the EagleLion in his pocket and took him home. This was the ultimate compromise formation. William's ability to not destroy, but rather care for EagleLion, illustrated just how much he had grown from this therapeutic process of working through a goodbye. Indeed, I was astonished by my little patient's resilience. Despite his anger and will to fight, he had a remarkable ability to internalize our relationship and find a solution that did not kill off himself, me or our shared creation and love, the EagleLion.

The following session was our last. When I inquired about our friend, William said that EagleLion stayed in his room for the week and liked the food. "Some day he might want to move to your house but for right now he likes my house." "That sounds like a good plan," I said.

Though we had a formal goodbye at the end of this session, the exchange was really our last. In the end, William found a way to stay connected and survive the goodbye. That, in essence, was the treatment.

The Complexity of Time-Limited Therapy in Clinical Training

Endings and goodbyes were powerful in this case not only because of my countertransference to William but because they spoke to the general difficulty I was having as a trainee in a one-year training program with termination of cases that I felt were only just beginning. I had the fortunate experience of being able to work with patients for up to four years during my pre-doctoral training, an experience quite unique for clinicians in training positions in any mental health discipline. Even though we accomplished much in a short time, I knew that my treatment of William was ending before it had the chance to mature. I experienced guilt that I had engaged William in such a journey only to end it prematurely, just as his mother had left him so early on in their relationship when he was only beginning to know her.

During the year of my pre-doctoral internship, we had seminars about the clinical implications of termination. While these seminars were very helpful, I was told many times that we were doing a "piece of the work" in time-limited treatment with our patients. And yet, as someone who was psychodynamically trained and who thinks about clinical interactions through a lens of attachment and trauma, I knew that I was leaving William too soon. I knew that, had our treatment continued, it could help him transform his aggression and rage in a more longstanding way.

On the other hand, there is a clear clinical benefit of early termination. I knew that if we had not ended so prematurely, William would not have experienced yet another maternal loss so powerfully. A treatment that began with displaced aggression and a global need for control over his environment ended with a journey in which William was able to travel through the dark woods and reach a place where his aggression had a voice, had a story to tell and had a history of loss and sadness. Creating this narrative through EagleLion helped William better understand himself and his journey. It was this opportunity for working through and putting words and affect to the in vivo experience of being left that was the truly therapeutic experience for William. It was only through the killing of EagleLion, saying goodbye and then bringing him back, that William could begin to mourn his early losses.

Using play as a gateway, William was able to transform his aggression and see that underneath it was a longing for connection, a defensive maneuver around the anxieties of attachment and the anger that came with current loss and past loss. Thus, through the loss of having to say goodbye to each other, William was able to move closer to the anger he felt when his mother said goodbye to him so long ago.

Often in our lives we do not get the chance to say a real goodbye to people we care about: people are either gone from our lives too quickly or the pain of the goodbye prevents us from staying connected. William was able to have the experience of saying goodbye in a way that he had never had with his mother. In so many ways, this was the most therapeutic part of the treatment, and yet would not have been possible without the premature termination at the end of my training year. Had we not used those months leading up to the termination to process the goodbye and let William kill off and bring back the EagleLion, he would not have been able to use the treatment to work through his unconscious experience of being abandoned. Both William and I have EagleLion to thank for that.

Bibliography

Bram, A. (2010). The relevance of the Rorschach and the patient-examiner relationship in treatment planning and outcome assessment. *Journal of Personality Assessment*, 92(2), 91–115.

Gardner, R. A. (1973). On the seashore of endless worlds, children play. *Contemporary Psychoanalysis*, 9(2), 392–399.

Handler, L., & Hilsenroth, M. J. (1994). The use of a fantasy animal drawing and storytelling technique in assessment and psychotherapy. Paper presented at the Annual Meeting of the Society for Personality Assessment, Chicago.

Tuber, S. (2012). *Understanding Personality through Projective Testing*. Lanham, MD: Jason Aronson.

Tuber, S. & Caflisch, J. (2011). *Starting Treatment with Children and Adolescents: A Process-Oriented Guide for Therapists*. New York: Routledge.

Winnicott, D. W. (1969). The use of an object. *International Journal of Psycho-Analysis*, 50, 711–716.

Winnicott, D. W. (1971a). *Playing and Reality*. Tavistock Publications.

Winnicott, D. W. (1971b). Therapeutic Consultations in Child Psychiatry [Introduction]. In *Therapeutic Consultations in Child Psychiatry*. London: Hogarth Press and the Institute of Psycho-Analysis.

5

FINDING ONE'S SELF

Developing a Therapeutic Identity as a Beginning Therapist Doing Long-Term Work

Monique S. Bowen

My goal as a beginning therapist had been to remain objective and neutral so as not to get into trouble for making my patients and their problems worse. To me, this meant, "do no harm": just listen and stay out of the way until you really know what is happening. The challenge that came often in my early treatment cases had been to rein in my longing to perfect my listening: a simultaneous engagement and focus on the areas of inner struggle for my patients. After all, listening until you understand your patient and their conflicts is central to making a well-informed intervention that challenges an established idea or perspective, or some closely held notion. And yet what informs a therapist's ability to make an intervention (or an interpretation) is not our objectivism or attempts to maintain a clinically neutral stance. In fact, our patients come to us with the hope that we will listen to them with an open mind, that we will have educated thoughts and opinions about what is going on with them, and that we will, at moments, share our point of view with them. Clearly, an opinion is not all a therapist has to offer, but being impartial neither reflects the interest one has in the people one treats, nor does it acknowledge the personal bias one develops as one becomes invested in the outcomes of patients who have come to therapy in pain seeking help.

Despite the various theoretical considerations and recommended therapeutic interventions that I have been exposed to in my years of training, in my own treatment, in my nascent practice, and now in preparing to write this chapter, it has been the self-monitoring of my own associations to my patient's conflicts that has most influenced my technique and overall therapeutic identity to a degree beyond which I feel can accurately quantify. Over the last ten years, I have increasingly contemplated whether to acknowledge these associations as something more than simply a common experience all therapists share. However, deciding whether to disclose those experiences to our patients has confronted therapists of almost every theoretical orientation with particularly strong challenges to familiar ways of thinking and working. My gradual acceptance of the role of intersubjective experience in the therapeutic process has made it possible for me to admit, without too much embarrassment, how often I have felt deep identifications—for good or bad—with my patients. Giving additional attention and careful consideration as to how I might communicate my values, beliefs, and judgments has served as an important tool for engaging my patients based on my particular identifications with them, their struggles, and the people in their lives. Not without bias, in choosing to approach the range of feelings and conflicts these identifications stir, my sense is that I have grown to receive feelings of self-doubt, confusion, frustration, exhilaration, joy, fear, discomfort, boredom, loss, and more with greater ease over the course of each new treatment case.

This work is personal. The transferences arising from similarities between the patient's other significant relationships and the one between patient and therapist, as well as the countertransferences, which represent a two-way communication from the therapist to the patient about some previous or current experience with others, provide the therapist with an occasion to understand the patient more fully (Tansey and Burke, 1989). Renik (1996) writes that it is on the basis of our own personal histories and "emotional involvement" with the realities of our patients that we are able to contribute to and to impact the self-investigative process they have undertaken with us. I agree with Renik's assertion that neutrality does little to help the patient because it fails to capture the value of the uncommon dialectic inherent in the therapeutic relationship. Rather, it is in the ability of the therapist to understand empathically and then to engage the patient about those issues that challenge the patient most that the therapist stands to make the greatest contribution.

In this chapter, I explore my patient's (I will call him Aden) projections and my identifications with those feelings. Looking back, it was through that process that I became able to empathize with his experiences in life in the form of (1) my own self-doubt as a therapist; (2) confusion about what the work would be in the therapy and a feeling that I was missing something crucial because I was new to this work; and (3) hostility because I felt seduced into the role of the overbearing, hypercritical parental figure holding up a mirror to my patient, nudging him to consider his actions and motivations. In those moments, I felt as though I was on some errand not of my own design, acting in a predetermined role, with a set script, and with expected outcomes. Once I was able to regroup, I could see how desperate he felt to connect to others but also how much he yearned for some experience (and guidance) on how to make the "right" decisions. Aden's wish to have a playbook for living was so strong and so central to his relationships, including with me, that there was often little room for spontaneity and creativity in his life.

Aden, in the beginning

Aden, a 19-year old Jewish male of Southern Arabian descent, presented at the clinic with concerns about his school performance and an "emotional semester" that left him feeling like "he needed someone to talk to." At the time of the intake interview, he reported low mood, difficulty concentrating, low energy, weight loss, and insomnia—symptoms he described as stemming from the end of a months-long relationship with a young woman he met at school. He described worries he had that "everyone will think I am a bad person," and stated that he had a number of intrusive thoughts about sex, in addition to repeated fantasies about being a superhero, or a member of the British and Israeli Secret Intelligence Services that he found difficult to interrupt given the intense level of enjoyment he got from his entertaining fantasy life. Aden's complaints also included an inability to focus on his schoolwork, and he expressed concerns about his ability to finish out the semester given his expectation of performing poorly on his final exams.

My early experiences with Aden were that he projected two self-images: one, as a lovesick college student motivated to seek therapy to discuss the relationship and how to perform better in school; and the other, as an affectively superficial and emotionally immature adolescent who expressed his feelings largely in terms of bodily distress—"It really hurts." "My body is so weak; I'm losing strength everyday." "I'm breaking down . . . what'll be next?" After Aden's evaluation with the clinic psychiatrist, his symptoms were viewed as a generalized anxiety, resulting from a limited capacity to handle stressors associated with balancing school, familial, and social demands. With initial concerns about a prodromal, pre-psychotic period allayed after consultation with a psychiatrist, the intake therapist gave a diagnosis of Adjustment Disorder (with one rule-out, Mood Disorder Not Otherwise Specified) on Axis I and Schizotypal Disorder on Axis II, and stated that he could be assigned to psychotherapy.

And so, therapy with Aden and supervision with my adult case supervisor commenced. In our clinic, it was not unusual for new clients over the age of 18 years old to be assigned as adult cases. As a result, my conceptualization of Aden's presenting problem and of the beginning treatment was much influenced by setting up the case as an adult treatment. After numerous conversations about his personality style with my then clinical supervisor, we utilized our understanding of schizoid character to frame my initial outlook on Aden's problems and to direct my early therapeutic actions. He exhibited infantile ideas of, and longing for, omnipotence that had not been outgrown and, thus, he continued to have substantial problems with regulation of his self-esteem. Aden reported that people experienced him as being dishonest about what he expected from his relationships with friends, family members, and potential female partners. He actively used his few relationships for his own gratification; he could not fully understand and consider others' interests. Furthermore, he described his friends mostly through self-comparisons, describing only the envy and anger he felt when they attained something he had not, with no comprehension of their difficulties, or perspectives on what their actual experiences might have been. Thus, those initial months of the treatment brought about a slight (though significant) evolution to our initial concern about a psychotic (schizotypal) process in Aden; what emerged instead was more schizoid in organization than the impairments to reality testing typical of more severe psychopathology.

Aden cited ongoing difficulties with his academic and social functioning, as well as a lack of purpose to his actions and a "blank feeling" that concerned him because "it ha[d] always been there." I was struck by how rarely he spoke about his relationships with others. His descriptions of his family members were sparse and lacked detail, such that it was often difficult to know if he was talking about his mother or father, or one of his siblings when he said 'he' or 'she.' First names were usually absent, so pronouns were sometimes my only hint as to whom or to what he was referring, which left me with the sense that the people in his life were interchangeable or, rather, viewed as the same. In those moments, I became aware of his feelings of loneliness and of isolation from others, and this was also reflected in his vague descriptions of people and his relationships. He was able to acknowledge his inability to relate to others, to understand other perspectives and motivations, and that others often found him distant, cold, and indifferent. He expressed wishes to be more popular but realized some of his own limitations in getting there, and that others still perceived him as "weird." As he slowly began to let me see how much he struggled to relate, I came to recognize that what lay beneath this presentation was a terrified young man who expressed suspicion in the face of feelings of emptiness, unacknowledged rage, and fears of being attacked by others.

Aden's main coping strategy had been to diminish any experiences of anger, confusion, or terror. As expected, my early attempts to point out, or discuss, these feelings were met with blank stares, silence, and the occasional "I don't know." However, what Aden could do was invite me into his world by descriptions of events, such as those surrounding his father's departure from the family and from Yemen. Most Jewish families in Yemen had departed the mostly Arab Muslim country in late 1940s, and a travel ban had remained in place until the early 1990s. Once the ban was lifted, Aden's father left to better his opportunities for work, first in Israel and then later the USA. He indicated that his father's departure forced his mother into the workforce for the first time, while she also shouldered the responsibilities of parenting her two young children alone and with little support. Worse still, Aden described an impoverished relationship with an older sibling, whose unidirectional aggressive feelings allowed him to recast himself in the role of sole victim of his sibling's sadism.

Aden indicated that he only saw his father every few years until he turned ten years old. He reported that his mother left about this time to join his father in Israel, while the children remained with relatives for several months until his parents could send for them. Once the family was in the same country again, Aden indicated that the full reunification was delayed, as they were unable to live all together for some time. He explained that there was not enough room to accommodate them all and that they may have lived separately for the six to nine months they were in Israel. Aden noted that the family only began living together under the same roof once they had made the journey to the northeast United States shortly before his twelfth birthday. He stated that for the first time he could detect the palpable tension between his parents, and that he and his sibling failed to bond with their father, much to his father's apparent disappointment.

He tried, but . . . it's hard to ask for a sudden [re-] connection to just happen. I think he knows but he just keeps busy with his work . . . so we still never see him. I mean, it's just like before [after his father left Yemen for Israel], except we all live together now.

The early treatment with Aden focused on several themes: his inability to identify his own wants and desires as separate from those expectations his parents possessed; whether he could perform academically and professionally at the level others seemed able to; his vacillating perception of himself as alternately powerful with the ability to accomplish all tasks set before him and to maintain "a top position" vis-à-vis others; and his view that he seemed to have little control over how he performed in relation to his peers and to his own expectations. Aden was often anxious and worried about when he would regain the status he believed he once had in the world. He defended against these self-criticisms by maintaining an often skewed and unrealistic perception of himself as a high-achiever. Thus, when he experienced any event that suggested he could reach his goals of infinite power, fortune, and fame—similar to the Caucasian male characters that occupied his fantasy world, including spies and superheroes—his self-esteem rocketed, endowing him with the ego inflation necessary to counteract his self-image as an under-achiever and a weakling.

His vulnerability and dependence upon me and on the treatment were also defended against, mostly in an effort to regulate his affective experiences and to exhibit some sense of control over himself and over me. In the midst of a given enactment, he continued to project self-sufficiency and, at times, would act as his own therapist, attempting to solve his own predicaments without my support and input. Yet, there were also those occasions when he seemed less sure of himself, when he sought approval for following my advice and he awaited praise for having done something in support of the treatment goals. It was in those moments that I was able to speak to his wish not to be chiefly responsible for his own care. Though the occasions when I was able to speak were short-lived, I think he could see that I wanted to help him, even if it remained difficult for him to allow me to care for him and thus release himself from his own self-mothering functions.

Though I acknowledged Aden's presenting problems as, in part, developmental (along a trajectory toward normal adult development) and having to do with his early object relations (pre-oedipal in origin but affected greatly by his affective and cognitive experiences across childhood and adolescence), this achievement was largely academic, even philosophical, as it was unclear where to go with this in conceptualizing the early treatment. Prior to Aden, I was used to patients sitting cross-legged under tables, dressing up as chefs and feeding me pies made from clay as they portrayed and attempted to resolve their phase-specific conflicts. Achieving mastery and solving problems through the adventure and risk of card and board games, and the meaningful communication and social interaction born of parallel crayon drawings, made sense to me in my therapy work with children and early adolescents. Despite an awareness of his stuck-ness and fragile sense of self, I lost sight of him as a mid to late adolescent and joined the clinic and my supervisor in interpreting his behaviors, gestures, and metaphors as those of a young adult man. Having overlooked this critical matter of his developmental phase was not the only misstep I would make but it was likely the first one, and this conceptualization came to inform the treatment proper, and shaped my earliest interactions with Aden and my thoughts on how to proceed in the therapy.

Early Treatment

In the first year, my work with Aden had been largely about naming his feelings and the dread that went along with the isolation, loneliness, and withdrawal from the world he experienced. I believed Aden's projections of worthlessness, helplessness, confusion, and anger were feelings that represented obstacles to his forming a coherent self-identity. Instead, through the therapy, I offered a nurturing, therapeutic relationship, as a counterpoint to some of the destructive patterns of his early childhood experience. By working through the transference relationship, my conscious hope was to supply some of the affective mirroring that had been missing from his experience. There were aspects of his experience as a young Jewish male immigrant of Arabian descent that seemed so far from my life as an African American woman; however, that did not halt my efforts to act as the better mother to this boy who seemed hungry for parental love and attention. Under the transactional pull of the transference-countertransference milieu, it took many months for me to appreciate the powerful wishes I had to best and (metaphorically) replace his real mother.

As his primary parental substitute, Aden had a laundry list of things to go over with me: he had questions about his masculinity, his sexuality, his intellectual ability, his integrity, and his purpose in life. These concerns suffused the treatment with complex biological and psychosocial matters that were difficult to explore without concordant feelings of despair and hopelessness. "Who am I? Who should I be? What should I be like with others? Who am I to you, and who are you going to be me in my life?" Behind those queries, I read his fears about whether I could be someone who helped him understand his experiences in the world. In addition to an empathic connection to Aden around some of his basic questions, I experienced the complement—a countertransferential reaction of feeling confused, frustrated, and irritated by his lack of agency and involvement in exploring these issues. I often felt as though understanding, processing, and working through these issues was more important to me than to him, and that the tasks of thinking and sharing ideas and opinions were one-sided. I found it challenging to avoid enactments with Aden as his main defensive stance often entailed putting me on the spot either by overvaluing my "expert opinion," or devaluing my interpretations as useless or immaterial. I, too, vacillated between feeling inadequate with this patient while also wanting to understand and relate to him. Sometimes I struggled in those early months to empathize with Aden, as he lacked the language to connect and speak to his feelings of loss. Looking back, I felt alone in making sense of his past experiences and of naming feelings I had imagined were connected to them. Really, how do you suggest someone mourn for that which has yet to be acknowledged as a loss?

By this time, I had been pregnant for the bulk of the treatment to date and I struggled mightily with any possibility of discussing my pregnancy with Aden. Still early in my training and now 12 weeks pregnant, I decided that since it was not obvious to him it had no immediate relevance. In retrospect, it had been very difficult for me to manage the impact of my pregnancy on me as a beginning therapist. For the sake of this new treatment and my own stable sense of self, it seemed easier to leave this life-changing event largely unexplored. Yes, I had begun to discuss this developing issue with my then supervisor, but much of our time and effort was spent helping me to empathize with how hard it was for Aden to be in the treatment room with me, pregnant or not. Aden was having such a difficult time being in a relationship with me and, frankly, I was having a similar experience. Managing my shifting roles and conflicts about them while simultaneously keeping his needs in mind was intense and, as a result of these most immediate concerns, the fact of my pregnancy was not broached until I was well into my sixth month. When I finally declared I was expecting a child, he had an appropriately difficult time incorporating this news about me. Aden expressed surprise at this information and quickly asked, "did you know all this time that you were pregnant?" When I answered affirmatively, he wondered aloud why I had waited to inform him. He probed gently about my secret, and my wish to keep aspects of my life private quickly gave way to feelings of shame for hiding too much from him. I felt rescued when he seemed satisfied with my response that it was not information that had had immediate bearing on the treatment but now that I was further along in my pregnancy, the reality of the impending birth was going to mean we would have to stop working together for a brief period of time. My explanations and excuses suffused the session and I left little room to discuss his reaction, which directly impacted our empathic tie. Rather than leave space to explore his experience of my pregnancy, I thought I could keep his projections at bay—at least, for a little while. In retrospect, I misunderstood this exchange with Aden and the importance of having an opportunity to talk with me about this experience was preempted. I got concrete, quickly: we discussed that there would be two scheduled interruptions in the treatment—a month-long clinic holiday followed shortly thereafter by my three-month maternal leave of absence from the clinic. In no time, I had to say good-bye to him and I honestly felt as though I had not prepared him.

During my leave of absence, Aden was assigned to a brief supportive therapy with another clinician. With the guidance of the clinic director and my clinical supervisor, I arranged for him to have these sessions with my male colleague. The decision to have Aden meet twice monthly with a therapist allowed him to maintain a positive connection to the clinic in my absence, while also not leaving it only up to him to request a therapeutic intervention if the need arose.

Upon my return, Aden let me know that I was missed while sharing with me the distinct value he placed on "those other sessions," as it allowed him to continue to have a relationship with the clinic and, in his words, "was a way to keep me coming back." He had made a connection to the interim therapist, and spoke of how much it meant to

> have him to talk to. I know it wasn't supposed to replace therapy like the way we talk to each other, but I don't have "guy talk" much and he knew what I was going through, and I could relate to him.

I came to understand Aden's anxious-aggressive demands about the break as an expression of his unformulated fears about therapy and of becoming close to me. It had been so difficult (I would imagine it felt very dangerous) for him to believe he could rely on me as a consistent presence. His underlying insecurity extended from his relationships with his parents, and a fear that people could not be reliably present. Thus, he doubted whether it made sense to ever count on anyone. His initial questions about that break in the treatment could be understood as part of a powerful wish to end the treatment—a definitive statement of rejection of me and closeness to me that was beginning to emerge as I came closer to understanding his anger, his fear, and the counterbalancing quality of his aggression and anxiety. Although I had shown myself to be available, giving him ample notice prior to absences or breaks, and informing him about changes to my schedule that impacted our session times, his experience of me—like significant others in his life—was still that I might not come back. *You left me alone to be with your baby and I had to survive without you. And even though you left someone in your place, I had to make do without you, and I am prepared for it to happen again.* "Affective states that were never attuned to will be experienced alone, isolated from the interpersonal context of shareable experiences." (Vanaerschot, 2004)

Aden's initial reaction after I returned from leave was to describe his session time with my male colleague, in part, as filling in a gap that I could not as a female therapist, which left me feeling undervalued for not being the preferred object choice. His reaction could also be seen as the result of feeling undervalued by me, as I withheld aspects of my experience that would ultimately impact the course of treatment. And yet I returned and so Aden's conflict—his basic mistrust of others as benevolent figures—was both enacted and challenged in the context of our ongoing treatment relationship. Although he worried about whether there was anyone else who would care enough about him to talk about the difficult things that we discussed, I think that he maintained a private hope that there could be someone else to relate to who might even understand him on another level, different from what I had offered him. The reframing of his abandonment feelings prior to breaks as evoking similar feelings of terror he experienced as a child, when both his parents were largely unavailable to him, began to help him access the anger, loss, and deprivation their early absences and separations generated. In many ways, his reactions were aligned with those of most teens on the cusp of an emergence into late adolescence, mounting "the process by which they come to see themselves more and more as young adults, and less and lees as their younger adolescent selves" (Levy-Warren, 1996, p. 106).

My experience in the consulting room with Aden reaffirmed this observation: he was able to gather momentary strength from my belief that the treatment and our work together would continue to help him understand his feelings of dread, isolation, and emptiness. And yet, that momentum was fleeting. Once his invigoration had dissipated, he was quick to devalue the treatment as ineffective, and to find me to be "less than helpful" as compared to the relationship experts he consulted in books, on-line, and in person and from whom he received the immediate bursts of stimulation his ego so desperately needed.

Summers (2000), like Khan (1964) and Winnicott (1965), emphasizes that failures in the early environment that impinge upon the evolution of self can mirror strains on the therapeutic relationship between patient and therapist, either as part of a transference repetition or in navigating a new possibility for the relationship. Khan proposes that the infant-child develops multiple self-states (1964) to compensate for the premature loss of dependency within the maternal relationship, and simultaneously to maintain some connection—albeit primitive—to the mother. Like Winnicott (1956), Khan writes that the mother who is unable to meet the infant's needs with an appropriate response falls short in fulfilling her role as the "protective shield and auxiliary ego" (Khan 1964, p. 272) for her infant child. This failure to accommodate the needs of the infant frustrates his attempts to gain confidence and trust both in his mother and the surrounding environment as consistently available and reliable. Khan's observations take on special resonance, given the ambivalence that was at the core of Aden's conflicts—how to trust that you can expect closeness with another while also concealing a significant fear of being rejected for seeking closeness?

Rather than solely conceiving of the therapy process as the working through of internal conflict and the interpretation of unconscious process, object relations theorists also see it as transformative of one's self-concept (Summers, 2000). Wile (1984) argues that early approaches often viewed patients as "seeking infantile gratifications, functioning at a regressed level, and resisting therapy" (p. 355). He (Wile, 1984) advocates striving for interpretations that speak not to the aggressive or regressed aspects of patients but instead to the longings for relationship, and deprivations of development, of needs that still need to be met. "People engage in offensive, exaggerated, 'infantile' expressions when they are unable to express important feelings and to feel that these feelings are understood by the other" (p. 360). For Wile (1984), interpretation need not be abandoned in working with such patients, but instead be carefully formulated to assure the patient that they are approved of and that the relationship is still intact. Wile (1984) maintains:

> [The problem with accusatory interpretations] is clients are already accusing themselves, often for the very thing the therapist is accusing them and that this—self-criticism—is the problem. [Once the] therapist recognizes clients are deprived, stuck, inhibited, and self-critical, they will attempt interventions, in contrast to the accusatory interpretations of the traditional approach, that will be inherently reassuring to clients.
>
> *(p. 363)*

Like Wile, Khan (1960) believed the real help we offer our patients comes in providing an environment (the analytic, or therapeutic, setting) where an approximation of the patient's experience of their early mothering can be explored and re-constructed, such that an important delineation can occur: separating the individual patient's primitive, psychic fantasy of mother and the relationship with mother from the pathologic external reality. Without help with this important achievement of self–object differentiation, followed by the necessary integration of one's experience into a coherent representation, the course of healthy, normal development is postponed.

Thus, my believing in this line of theory prompted an important adjustment to my work with this patient: to appreciate and to engage the role of vivid fantasy in his life. Aden was someone who preferred fantasy over reality—editing his real life events so that they turned out as he might have imagined rather than accepting the actual outcomes. Given his inclination to fantasize about all aspects of his life, I found that I had multiple opportunities to observe Aden in his world—at school, at work, at play, and at rest. For reasons that I credit to my own ease with reverie and to my experience exploring these issues with keen interest in supervision, I felt well suited to work with his fantasy material. Rather than be hypercritical of the amount of time he spent in various dissociated states, my eagerness and theoretical stance allowed me to be more open and receptive to his processes of living his life, his ways of understanding and relating to others (albeit limited at times), and his capacities of coping with frustrations and disappointments.

Year II: Emergence of Reverie and Its Uses in Therapy and Supervision

In my first year as a beginning therapist working with young children, I kept secret that I dreamt about my therapy cases. To be more exact, I hid not only the fact but also the frequency of my dreams. My waking dreams were more prevalent, in the form of daydreams, interior thoughts, and attention toward stirring visual stimuli evoked by session material. When I was pregnant and sleepiness would shudder my brain, despite having had a peaceful night of sleep, I assumed I was to blame for being overtired rather than to allow that perhaps the session content might be reason to steer my mind away from interest and fascination and instead toward somnambulism. My great shame as a beginner was the degree to which my early cases seemed prey to this focal restlessness—an unwelcomed counterpart to what seemed unlike the descriptions of the analytic third ear and that stood to erode my nascent clinical sense of self.

Both supervisors for my therapy with Aden noted a quality to my verbatim notes when I seemed to lose my empathic tie to my patient. Like my experience of Aden from our sessions, I found that in supervision my remarks were leaden, garrulous, and without mooring. I could not describe accurately what led up to my interventions nor would I admit that barometric changes in my descriptions of the treatment were due to the swell of confusion brought out by reveries. After their careful and repeated efforts to free me of my excessive self-reproach, my attempts to conceal finally gave way to disclosures of self–other experiences with and about my patient. Once I could share most of my conscious thoughts and impressions of Aden in supervision, I found I was able to articulate myself in the first person and with some self-approval for not shutting off a potentially useful aspect of the countertransference.

In listening to Aden in sessions, I typically had a posture of following him visually on whatever journey he shared with me in a given session. As he described his experiences, endeavors, fantasies, and errands, I tried to accompany him as though in the action myself. Equipped with film and literary references from most of our early sessions, I was poised to learn more about the superhero inhabitants with whom Aden most identified. These "grown-ups" figured prominently in his imagination and I came to believe that understanding their public and private personas might offer insight into his secreted life. I read about these men with whom he connected, sought advice from peer experts about identifications with certain characters and their superhuman strengths, and considered the traits he chose to model based on these überhuman (unrealistic) representations. Three storylines emerged that would serve as helpful guideposts over the course of the treatment: (1) the myth of metamorphosis (Packer, 2009) common to superhero stories provided Aden with a secure, narrative structure from which to assimilate an American identity and to project an emerging masculinity replete with conflicted sexual urges; (2) Aden's most idealized heroes are born of affluence and project self-sufficiency, until they suffer some medical setback that requires a technological intervention to strengthen them physically but that expose their human vulnerabilities; and (3) his heroes have internal demons which they seek to transform by way of chemical or surgical intervention or, in some cases, by entering "recovery"—some form of therapeutic intervention or self-help group—to find answers that have eluded them.

I think because of my receptivity to what at one time was an adaptive response to his childhood and adolescent experience of isolation and rejection, Aden and I were able to discuss the role that fantasy has had in maintaining the disconnections he felt from friends, family members, and acquaintances. His flights into fantasy had a far-reaching impact, making it difficult for him to tolerate even minimal frustrations without seeking a withdrawal from reality. Modell (1975) writes that these patients have an early experience of their caregivers as not fully capable of fulfilling their needs, and as a result they deny the parent (Modell refers to the mother) as a loving and benevolent object. Though Aden could acknowledge how his fantasy life served him in his daily living, the other associated affects of his particular parental relationships, chiefly the anger and hatred he felt toward them along with the overwhelming wish he had to feel valued and understood by them, were rejected and powerfully defended against in reality. For example, in the face of disappointments Aden recounted numerous instances of putting himself into trance-like states where he was able to

> re-live recent events in my life and put my own spin on them. Control them and have them end the way I want. I can't even tell you—you wouldn't even believe how much time I am there, doing that. It's basically all of the time. I mean like it would have to be 90 percent of the time.

Bollas (1983) writes that it is through the reliving of the patient's infant life in the transference, and through the "freely roused emotional sensibility [that the therapist] welcomes news from within himself (p. 2)," that brings the unconscious derivatives of psychoanalytic work into awareness as the associative material of the countertransference experience. By maintaining access to our internal potential space (Winnicott, 1974), Bollas (1983) argues, and I agree, that we create a countertransference readiness open to accepting the patient's transference communication, and in turn the patient constructs an environment where the patient and therapist can reside—the therapist in a "not knowing yet an experiencing" (p. 4) state, and the patient in a state of communicating his self- and object-representations, as well as for the unconscious discovering of the therapist's use (as an object).

His fixation with this activity was incredibly gratifying, and so any difficulties that resulted from his passionate devotion to it were acceptable, so long as he kept this thing that he so relied upon for sustenance. He derived short bursts of energy from the self-confidence his secret world provided, and the roles (e.g. the leader of a vast army, an arrogant hunk who is indifferent to others but beloved by men and women alike for his confidence and charm) he inhabited there allowed him to feel powerful and special when in reality he often felt insignificant or—even worse for him—ordinary.

The conscious turning inward into fantasy was understandable given his experience of his parents as rejecting figures—coping with both his mother's general lack of physical and emotional availability, and his father's protracted absences and emotional cut-off once the family was later reunited. This defensive stance, which protected Aden from feelings of inadequacy and frightening affective states, satisfied his honest desire to be a highly effective adult, and his powerful wish to manipulate situations to his benefit and to remove the limits posed by reality.

> The patient develops a character structure and object-relating pattern that provides a modus vivendi with the world, while protecting [the patient] from further disappointment. Instead, an internal, narcissistically defined projective object develop[s]. . . . This object has two aspects: It can be pleased by the patient's efforts, but it is also hated and feared. As a result, the patient never brings about an experience of real success and self-esteem enhancement. To do so would be to admit the need for a real object.
>
> *(Almond, 2004)*

Though he rarely maintained an entrenched stance with me in the treatment around adhering to his rules, he did resort to some fantasy notion about what he wished others would do, what he might coerce others to do for him, and what he could re-create in fantasy such that a given scenario would unfold the way he liked. Aden attempted to thwart the reality of external limitations with the activation of an omnipotent psychic framework that was employed to justify why he was exempt from the limits others accepted with greater ease. I interpreted his efforts to control aspects of his real-life interactions, and through his fantasy life, as an attempt to create distance in his relationships, including with me. I suggested that perhaps the day would come when he could shed this frame and welcome one not pre-set, where the outcomes were most welcomed because they were unexpected.

I attempted to illustrate this with Aden by willfully shifting our fantasy talk to another of Aden's favorite topics, one we shared: Basketball. At six feet tall, I love basketball and this typically has been misunderstood as a personal longing for my "playing days." My height, combined with knowledge of the sport and a willingness to engage in long conversations about it, has caused men and women alike to make this common, though false, juxtaposition. At first, Aden believed he would have to explain the game to me. When I was in my "early blank screen" phase, I said little when he would tell me about pick-up games he was involved in, or on those rare, yet lovely moments, when he would recount highlights from the previous night's match-ups. When I was pregnant and feeling largely unnoticed by Aden, any interruption of his narration of the games was ignored, or met with a smile I recognized as self-satisfaction: *Listen, lady. I'm trying to teach you something. So listen up!* And, I did mostly listen, as that was my job after all. Except those times, when I would muse about those same plays he described, that I actively processed those unseen coaching decisions that cost one team or the other the win. I appreciated having an opportunity to think about the back-and-forth of Aden's pick-up games—to imagine him on court, managing his self-declared role as the two-guard, shooting from the outside whenever possible. Unfortunately though, Aden rarely envisioned the full court game and, therefore, he often missed opportunities to pass the ball to an open teammate, namely the other guard, or to dish the ball to the player in the post, closest to the basket. Though we discussed our mutual disdain for the selfish play by various shooting guards in professional basketball, in truth, Aden aspired to be like them. There was no denying how good it felt for him to identify as a scorer, and to be known by other players as able to make three-pointers with distance between him and the closest defender. I relate to him, and to the feeling.

For my part, now that I knew Aden's favorite spot on the court and that he played his position with little awareness of his teammates and where they were positioned to add to the offense, certain limitations on my role in the treatment room began to make more sense, too. To extend this metaphor a bit further, at the beginning of the treatment I acted more as a coach who thought I could help Aden most if I could extend his playmaking skills, adding ball-handling to his responsibilities and developing his ability to execute plays in the half-court. After my maternity leave from the clinic, I was able to acknowledge how restricted I was to the role of either encouraging or discouraging Aden's acquisition of new skills. Instead, I now believed I had to check in to the game as a fellow player. From this vantage point, I was able to share my view on the game and to model how to extend his view to include the next several plays rather than maintaining a singular focus on scoring. By becoming more active myself, I also became visible and my invitations to join me in being curious about the entire, full-court game had greater appeal. Furthermore, a shared space slowly emerged, one where we could leave our pre-set roles behind in favor of exploring what else might be possible for us, as members of the same team.

A Transitional Space of Our Own: For the Unknown Self, and the Foreign Other

At intermittent points in those eighteen months of therapy with Aden, I found myself very interested—sometimes tantalizingly distracted—by the lack of information Aden had shared about his life prior to immigrating to the United States. In the early months of the treatment, I wondered about the back story he presented—an ordinary family moves from an economically depressed country to the "land of plenty" where the family can lay roots and the children can grow, learn, and work in professions that greatly change the financial future for the family. Later, we discussed his immigration story—the major events he could recall, finer details that he had not given much thought to, and some of his subjective observations about his family's move from Yemen, through Israel, to the United States. In fact, given the Arab, Asian, and European influences on educated Yemeni Jews, it is possible that the impacts of immigration I assumed might be a part of his growing-up experience were mitigated by his class standing in his home country, and his family's metaphorical distance from the experience and beliefs of the early Jews or even the indigenous Arab people of Yemen. Later, with consistent prods spurred on by my curiosity, Aden provided a more complex description of his life in Yemen and Israel: a frequently absent father and emotionally distant mother, a sibling who acted out aggressively toward him, bullying at the hands of his same-aged peers, and an intense insecurity about his own academic and social intelligences.

Several months into the treatment, while recalling the difficult transitions to life in the US, he shared with me how negative the familial and interpersonal dynamics of his life were, and how, from his point of view, most aspects of life worsened post-immigration. He told me about an early incident at his then new middle school where he had been admonished by a teacher and his principal for infringing on the personal space of a classmate. In his home country, Aden had been accustomed to showing affection toward classmates, including male class-mates, with a hug or an arm around the shoulder. What once had been a casual and normal activity in his mind quickly became dangerous. He described his middle school classmate's reaction as angry and confused—"He told me to get off of him, not to touch him like that. I don't know. He was pretty mad, and looked [at me] like 'what are you doing?'" Aden said that he was pulled aside by his teacher and the principal and told not to touch anyone else—"She said, 'Keep your hands to yourself and things will be better that way.'"

Listening to Aden recall his first experiences at his school, in this country with its foreign customs, I immediately empathized with his feeling like an outsider, and how he may have experienced this admonishment as a way of isolating and separating him even more from his peer group as different, or alien. As the child of an African immigrant, I had many of my own experiences with my father of feeling separate from him and his country of birth, as well as of isolating him for not "knowing" something about being American. And yet there were also many ways that as part of my allegiance to my father, I also felt myself to be somehow different, an outsider in relation to certain cultural norms and customs. Listening to Aden, I related to his sense of feeling misunderstood by others and I recognized that I too did not understand the breadth of his immigrant experience. Akhtar (1995) has described the experience of immigration as "an adult life reorganiza-tion of the identity (p. 1053)." More than making a generic comparison between the separation and individuation process and that of immigration, Akhtar (1995) highlights the impacts on character of the psychic development of the immigrant. Though the psychological outcomes of immigration for immigrants are multi-determined—the impact of voluntary versus involuntary immigration; the pre-adolescent versus post-adolescent immigration; the mourned departure from the home country versus the maladaptive dissociation of the migration, to name a few factors—there is little argument that the transformative event of a permanent immigration represents a dislocation (Volkan, 1993). The questions surround the extent of the mourning and the acceptance of this major life change and its accompanying disruptions (Volkan, 1993).

As the newest person at his school, not to mention under-sized as compared to his peers, Aden experienced some of the harsher realities of the American school system and the social ways of being of his middle school peers. Settling into a new city with a starkly different ethnic, racial, and economic composition than his home city and country, in addition to the expectations that he acclimatize quickly to unfamiliar surroundings, set him apart from others and yet his desire to fit in with the other children kicked into gear. He reported adopting the mannerisms, interests and customs of his multi-ethnic American school and neighborhood peers. Akhtar (1995, p. 1062) describes the distance that exists on an external level between the immigrant's mother country (the "mother of symbiosis") and their newly adopted country of residence (the "mother of separation"), and on an internal level between an "ethnocentric withdrawal and counterphobic assimilation." Aden's parents insisted that the children hold tight to their customs, traditions, language, and food; however, outside the family there was a rejection of his cultural and national origins. From comics to creative slang phrases, basketball to hip-hop music, Aden sought to blend into the crowd of adolescents at his school and in his neighborhood, seeking a general social acceptance perhaps more so than even close friendship within his peer group. He chose his activities and other assumed characteristics carefully—wishing to fit in with the boys who teased and bullied him for displaying a softer disposition. His attempts to be viewed as masculine rather than as feminine, to be seen as an American and not as someone different from the rest, represented the distances he attempted to bridge in his dual separation and individuation process during the phases of his adolescence and in his identity as an immigrant to becoming a citizen of the USA. In order to "pass" as a typical, urban American teen rather than to be distinguished as the child of Arab (or ethnic Jewish) immigrants can be understood in Oedipal terms: Could his newly adopted American self-representation "win out" over his native self-representation?

In her 1999 article on the issue of identity in contemporary clinical theory, Leary considers the life of the essayist Anatole Broyard—outed by Henry Louis Gates as a man of African descent who had passed as Caucasian for most of his adult life—as a way of understanding the difficulty of developing one's identity in a society where the issue of one's race, class, or sexual orientation matters so much because of the socio-political agendas of individuals and communities. Though we are more accustomed in modern media to the disclosure of who is a gay man or a lesbian, the exposure of a hidden identity such as being of African descent, Jewish, non-Anglo Saxon, Southern, Republican, Democrat, social conservative, poor, wealthy, and so on has been a deep, rich, and sometimes perverse tradition in the United States.

As a means of losing the label of "soft," Aden instead tried to project an image of masculinity he considered sublime—a super-human hero who was to be revered by men and lusted after by women. He expressed limits in his ability to connect to his masculinity, though it was through these mythic proportions that he had been able to access the lore of masculinity, versus the reality and everydayness of being an ordinary man. For Aden, this image was not simply a representation of what it meant to be male; I believe there was the additional wish to connect to the powerful aggressors at whose whim he had felt subjected. This identification could be understood from different vantage points, including (1) in the form of the impact of centuries-long colonization and exploitation by Britain, the former Soviet Union, and other Arab states on the politically and economically vulnerable Yemen; (2) as an undersized boy feeling victimized by larger and more agentic adolescents; or (3) as the member of an ethnic minority who felt bested by the intimidating, and the equally stereotypical, dominant male establishment guy with the world at his fingertips. Aden had many concerns about his social, cultural, racial, and political capital and how it could be used to maintain a distorted self-image that allowed him to pass unnoticed in certain settings, and allowed him, at minimum, to feel as though he was accepted in others. Leary (1999) writes about the risk of public social persecution that comes with the taking on of false identities, and warns that many types of passing are common:

> [The identities] serve as powerful meditations on authenticity and social authority. They [narratives on passing] problematize identity and raise [questions] . . . to what extent is the experience of self and subjectivity a matter of performance, development, or constitutional endowment? Is passing only an act of duplicity or are we in some critical sense who we fashion ourselves to be?
> *(p. 94)*

As for hidden identities, Aden felt persecuted for being effeminate, and as a result he questioned his lack of sexual prowess with women as possibly linked to how women view him; he also wondered if perhaps he was not as interested in women as even he had suggested. He had not said that he was gay but he had reported asking himself "the question," and that he has not sought an answer to his own query. For Aden, being declared feminine, or considered gay, represented a risk to his identity in his family, and served as a reminder of that part of him—the softer, more emotionally vulnerable side—he wished to disavow.

During the course of the treatment, I stumbled around conversations related to the racial and ethnic differences that distinguished us, and how we represented ourselves to one another in the context of the treatment. Were we not both trying on identities and seeing to what extent the other would accept us in our self-defined roles? On the occasions when something relevant to either of our cultural or social backgrounds had arisen naturally, I had a much more thoughtful comment on its relevance and relationship to the material because the event was grounded in the transference relationship as I understood it. The times when I had more spontaneous responses to my associations to the material, I would first attempt a "contemplative silence" (Akhtar, 2013)—some time to consider whether I was responding more to my conflicts than to his, or to some superficial consideration of the differences between us. My wish was that it would instead be an acknowledgment of how our responses had as much to do with how separate and alone we both felt *as with any actual cultural differences*, and how highlighting these distinctions could represent a point of connection and closeness. In the literature on conducting culturally competent, multicultural treatments, Hwang (2006) states that it is agreed among researchers that it is more important that therapists develop cultural competence through exploration of their own cultural identities and the development of a cultural self awareness in an effort to be available to understand the impacts of culture on their clients' identities and awareness of self.

Throughout the course of my work with Aden, I left the broader realities of our racial, ethnic, and gender differences largely unexplored. I openly discussed each of these areas with Aden only in relation to his own experience with others, occasionally wondering aloud about the relative importance of these issues on the treatment. Yet, I rarely initiated direct conversations about its bearing on our work together. Conversely, these were the exact themes that I had brought to supervision as central and salient to the transference relationship and to my countertransference reactions to the patient and the treatment relationship. I felt largely unacknowledged and unrecognized by Aden as an individual, as a woman, a pregnant woman, a black woman, an American with a parent who immigrated to the US, and as a professional in a unique position to help him with his issues of selfhood.

With the consistent disavowal of my individualism and the separateness of my own thoughts, I often felt as though he should see someone with more experience, with more expertise to offer, with a more empathic stance, and with time (my maternity leave seemed to loom large for me when the treatment began). Someone, in fact, anyone but me seemed preferable. Perhaps, a male, I thought; he would take notice of, and listen to, a man because it was a father figure he really needed. A man could not get pregnant and abruptly leave him and the therapy in limbo just when he needed him most. These different issues converged to inform my particular relationship with Aden and provided a window to his transferences, and my feelings of inadequacy contained valuable information that gave me access to Aden's conflicts and defenses. Akhtar (1995) refers to the immigrant's psychosocial change process as a "state of psychic flux" (p. 1052) that brings about a third separation-individuation phase, similar experientially to the two other dynamic phases of development in that it marks a change process that sets in motion another aspect of our identity formation. Perhaps another point of salience for my patient is that his immigration to the US occurred on the cusp of his actual second process of individuation to adolescence. This poorly timed coupling of shifting developmental and demographic events, along with his entangled identification with his mother and his Oedipal rivalries with his father, may have subtly yet remarkably contributed to his difficulties with self presentation throughout his adolescence and into his early adulthood.

My subjective experience of Aden and his immigration experience informed our work during each phase of the treatment. I struggled to raise, and keep alive, issues of identity in the treatment room, and these factors were central issues I sought to consider, understand, and value. In the closing phase of our work together, Aden began to use our hours together to discuss openly the ways he struggled to hold onto aspects of his identity that seemed not to fit with Western definitions of masculinity. It was of central importance in helping bring into focus the influences of his cultural and historical past on his present relationships.

This was a remarkable treatment experience for me and I learned so much about myself as a beginning therapist in working with Aden. Despite the challenges, it was my honor to have had the opportunity to know, to treat, and to share in the development of this young man. I will forever hold onto the space we created together—in my mind and in my heart.

References

Akhtar, S. (1995). A third individuation: immigration, identity, and the psychoanalytic process. *Journal of the American Psychoanalytic Association*, 43, 1051–1084.

Akhtar, S. (2013). *Psychoanalytic Listening: Methods, Limits, and Innovations*. London: Karnac Books.

Almond, R. (2004). "I can do it (all) myself": Clinical technique with defensive narcissistic self-sufficiency. *Psychoanalytic Psychology*, 21(3), 71–384.

Bollas, C. (1983). Expressive uses of the countertransference—notes to the patient from oneself. *Contemporary Psychoanalysis*, 19, 1–33.

Hwang, W. C. (2006). The Psychotherapy Adaptation and Modification Framework: application to Asian Americans. *American Psychologist*, 61(7), 702–715.

Khan, M. M. R. (1960). Clinical aspects of the schizoid personality. *International Journal of Psychoanalysis*, 41, 430–436.

Khan, M. M. R. (1964). Ego distortion, cumulative trauma, and the role of reconstruction in the analytic situation. *International Journal of Psychoanalysis*, 45, 272–279.

Leary, K. (1999). Passing, posing, and "keeping it real." *Constellations*, 6(1), 85–96.

Levy-Warren, M. H. (1996). *The Adolescent Journey: Development, Identity Formation, and Psychotherapy*. Northvale, NJ: Jason Aronson.

Modell, A. H. (1975). A narcissistic defence against affects and the illusion of self-sufficiency. *International Journal of Psychoanalysis*, 56, 275–282.

Packer, S. (2009). *Superheroes and Superegos: Analyzing the Minds behind the Masks*. Santa Barbara, CA: Praeger.

Renik, O. (1996). The perils of neutrality. *Psychoanalytic Quarterly*, 65, 495–517.

Summers, F. (2000). The analyst's vision of the patient and therapeutic action. *Psychoanalytic Psychology*, 17, 547–564.

Tansey, M. and Burke, W. (1989). *Understanding Countertransference: From Projective Identification to Empathy*. Hillsdale, NJ: Analytic Press.

Vanaerschot, G. (2004). It takes two to tango: on empathy with fragile processes. *Psychotherapy: Theory, Research, Practice, Training*, 4(2), 112–124.

Volkan, V. D. (1993). Narcissistic personality disorder. *Journal of the American Psychoanalytic Association*, 41, 273–276.

Wile, D. B. (1984). Kohut, Kernberg, and accusatory interpretations. *Psychotherapy: Theory, Research, Practice, Training*, 21, 353–364.

Winnicott, D. W. (1956). On transference. *International Journal of Psychoanalysis*, 37, 386–388.

Winnicott, D.W. (1965). Ego distortion in terms of true and false self. In D. W. Winnicott, *The Maturational Processes and the Facilitating Environment*. New York: International Universities Press.

Winnicott, D. W. (1974). Fear of breakdown. *International Review of Psychoanalysis*, 1, 103–107.

6

MODELING A THERAPEUTIC IDENTITY FOR A BEGINNING THERAPIST IN SUPERVISION

Jenny Kahn Kaufmann

It is a pleasure to revisit this case that I supervised several years ago. Monique's thoughts on her work as a beginning therapist are complex and rich, and I will build upon her reflections with my own memories and descriptions of a few aspects of this case that resonate as particularly important to me in re-visiting this late adolescent treatment. My relationship with Monique was a very special experience for me because our collaboration both encompassed and surpassed the formative function of supervision as modeling and developing a therapeutic identity. As I will describe in this paper, the work we did together around processing race, class, and privilege challenged me to look at myself and at my implicit biases in ways that were uncomfortable for me but ultimately expansive and liberating. At the same time, I challenged her to see me in ways that went beyond her first impressions of me. I know that we both grew immensely from being challenged by one another, so that our defensive organizations became looser and more flexible and, in turn, that change was paralleled in the patient's ("Aden's") therapy with Monique.

Understanding Defensive Omnipotence

In my mind, Aden fits into a category that I think of as a case of defensive omnipotence. With Aden, there is a split between the archaic, shameful sense of self and the more ideal self that he hopes to project, as is reflected in his obsession with superheroes and in his frequent retreats into fantasy. These ideas come from theories of intersubjectivity, which posit that affective experience is regulated—or dysregulated—from birth onward within mutual systems of influence (Orange, Atwood and Stolorow, 1997; Beebe and Lachmann, 2002). An absence of steady, attuned responsiveness to the child's affect states leads to significant derailments of optimal affect integration, and to the child's propensity to dissociate or disavow affective reactions. It is in such derailments of affect integration that the inter-subjective roots of shame can be found. The child can feel ashamed of what he feels, and believes there's something shameful about having the sorts of intense reactions he experiences.

Because of these recurring experiences of misattunement and consistent experiences of unmet developmental yearnings and reactive feeling states to these rejections, the child acquires the unconscious conviction that he either has a loathsome defect or an inherent inner badness. To compensate for being bad, a defensive self-ideal is established. In Aden's case, we can see this ideal in his fantasies about being a super-hero or a member of the British and Israeli Special Intelligence. As he told Monique, he retreats to fantasy about 90 percent of the time. In his fantasies, he pulls on one of his mythic stories and heroes, and with a magical sleight of hand, replaces what actually happened in life with what he wished had happened. This becomes necessary because he cannot process what actually happened, and if he did, it would reinforce his sense of badness. Kohut (1977) writes that when the child's developmental strivings are met with massive traumatic deflations, the child has symptoms of narcissistic depletion—feelings of emptiness, deadness, and worthlessness. I believe that this is what Aden was experiencing when he came to the clinic with worries about being unable to focus on his schoolwork, feeling unable to finish out the semester, and complaints that his body felt weak and that he was losing strength every day.

Another aspect of cases where the patients manifest defensive omnipotence is that patients strive to believe that they are self-sufficient, and cannot allow themselves to rely on anyone. They are terribly ashamed of their dependency needs, and so one of the most difficult aspects of treatment has to do with establishing trust. For Aden, he had such an expectation of being criticized, ridiculed, or otherwise deflated by a caregiver that he held back aspects of himself, and acted in ways that brought about the very outcomes that he likely feared most. At times, Monique felt herself being pulled into the role of a critical caregiver and she struggled to understand how this came about. She writes,

> . . . I felt seduced into the role of the overbearing, hypercritical parental figure holding up a mirror to my patient, nudging him to consider his actions and motivations. In those moments, I felt as though I was on some errand not of my own design, acting in a predetermined role, with a set script, and with expected outcomes.

(p. 48)

Despite getting pulled into these enactments, Monique was able to regroup, and learned to appreciate how desperate Aden felt to connect to others. Once she realized that she had been pulled into an enactment and found herself to be acting out of character, she was able to remind herself how desperate Aden was feeling to connect to others, and was able to speak to him respectfully, in a way that kept his terror, desperation, and vulnerability in mind.

I did understand Aden's character organization as schizoid, in that he seemed to seek refuge from a hostile, external world (Fairbairn, 1940). In trying to understand how he became this way, I worked with Monique to consider such ideas as the difference between developmental and defensive omnipotence. From my perspective, developmental omnipotence is a natural state of events that occurs during the child's second year of life. Drawing on theorists such as Mahler and Stern, this period includes the development of the intersubjective and narrative selves: a time when the young toddler feels she possesses unlimited power and resources and, in effect, believes, "the world is my oyster." One of the many jobs of parents is to meet their child's grandiosity, while also helping the child to build a more realistic sense of self, and helping them to cope with gradual disillusionments along the way (Brandchaft, 1993). When development goes awry, the child will not have a healthy sense of self and, thus, will be more likely to develop defensive grandiosity—a difficulty taking the needs and feelings of others into account and an oversized sense of self to compensate for corresponding feelings of deficiency.

Another aspect in cases of defensive omnipotence is that patients often look to their therapists as people who can give them all the answers about the right way to live. These are people who have been objectified by their caregivers and, thus, view themselves and others as objects. At times, they may also look to their therapists as the idealized "experts," while at other points they may devalue therapists as worthless with nothing to offer them. I believe that we articulated the problem well, which was an important prerequisite towards holding onto a realistic sense of how her patient was able to make early use of her in the treatment situation. Aden certainly challenged Monique in this way, vacillating between overvaluing her "expert opinion" and devaluing her interpretations as "useless or immaterial" (p. 53). These vacillations are challenging for any therapist, and especially difficult for a beginning therapist.

Therapeutic Action

Monique draws on different authors to help her understand therapeutic action, including—but not limited to—Masud Khan (1964) and Christopher Bollas (1983). Monique reminds us that Aden is plagued by his feelings of dread, isolation, and emptiness. On a deep level, he feels there something is wrong with him—he feels ashamed for being somehow bad, or defective, and that it is his own damn fault for being this way. Thus, the therapeutic questions become (1) how to show Aden where these awful feelings originated from—in part, to interrupt the level of responsibility he feels—so that he can stop blaming himself, and (2) how to explore with him how he became imprisoned for a crime he did not commit. Somehow, it means pulling Aden out of the force-field of the trauma, so he can see it from some distance.

According to Khan (1964), the way out of this dilemma is to recreate a therapeutic environment where the patient has a window into the earliest conditions of his own life. By separating his fantasy of an omnipotent, benevolent mother who met all his needs from the reality of an early mothering situation where he was insufficiently attended to, neglected, or abandoned, the patient can begin to see that there is a reason why he feels so depleted and empty. It is not because there is something inherently wrong with him, or because there is something bad or faulty within the self. Once the patient can begin to separate the "primitive, psychic fantasy of mother and the relationship with mother from the pathologic external reality" (Khan, 1964), then he can begin to form a coherent self-representation. The patient can then begin to distinguish between self and others, to trust his own perception and in some fundamental way, begin to inhabit his very own self. As a result, the individual starts to develop a coherent, integrated sense of self and agency, and as Monique writes, "without help with this important achievement of self–object differentiation, followed by the necessary integration of one's experience into a coherent representation, the course of healthy, normal development is postponed" (p. 56). Here, I would like to add that when all goes well, the course of development is postponed until there are conditions that allow the individual to open up; otherwise, the patient is in danger of stagnating.

Despite how preoccupied Monique would feel with Aden, her "first-born," when she was separated from him, the experience of being in the room with Aden was a different matter altogether. It seemed as if no matter how well rested Monique was when going into the room with him, it did not take long before her brain turned "away from interest and fascination and instead toward somnambulism" (p. 57). When Monique tried to wake herself up by making a comment or interpretation, she found her session responses to be "leaden, garrulous and without mooring" (pp. 57). I agree that she was way too hard on herself, but it was only by acknowledging her sense of shame and humiliation to her supervisors, and having them respond to her kindly and without reproach, that Monique was able to stop excoriating herself, tell her supervisors what had been going on in her mind, and begin to regain her sense of self. In her words, "Once I could share most of my conscious thoughts and impressions of Aden in supervision, I found I was able to articulate myself in the first person" (p. 67).

Monique also raises an excellent question about how to help Aden out of a merger with his idealized mother, in which he cannot see her or himself clearly. Consequently, Aden cannot seem to get a grip on his own sense of self as a separate being. Like a mother who is engaged in primary maternal preoccupation, Monique takes in Aden, and realizes she is thinking about him much of the time, at times landing on the topic of him outside their sessions. In much the same way that Loewald (1977) has in mind when he writes about primal density, Monique and Aden become mixed up with one another too. She reports feeling a sense of shame about how involved she was with her early therapy cases, for not only did she dream about Aden at night, she also mused during the day to a "degree to which my early cases seemed prey to [a] focal restlessness" (p. 57). I think this illustrates how Monique had to let herself get all tangled up with her patient, and then trust her supervisors enough to be able to use them, so as to work her way out of the Monique–Aden merger. We too had to help her work her way out of the identification she was feeling with him in order to regain her sense of authority. It represents a great example of the self-object differentiation that Khan advocates.

Monique also draws upon the work of Christopher Bollas (1983) in her thinking about the case. Like Khan (1964), Bollas (1983) also believes in grasping the importance of early infant life, and working it through in the transference/countertransference matrix. Monique quotes Bollas (1983) as saying that it is

> through the reliving of the patient's infant life in the transference, and through the "freely roused emotional sensibility that the therapist welcomes news within himself" that brings the unconscious derivatives of psychoanalytic work into awareness as the associative material of the countertransference experience.
>
> *(p. 58, this volume)*

Monique goes on to say that being in a state of countertransference readiness helped her to appreciate the role of vivid fantasy in her patient's inner life. On the one hand, she sees his retreat into fantasy as an adaptive response to his childhood and adolescent experience of isolation and rejection; on the other hand, she wants Aden to understand that this mode of coping with frustrations and disappointments was maladaptive, and was keeping him disconnected from his friends, family members, and acquaintances.

Reading my supervisee's thoughts on these issues makes me wonder whether it can sometimes be confusing to apply psychoanalytic ideas to these early psychotherapy cases. When Bollas (1983) works with cases psychoanalytically, he tries to recreate the conditions of early infant life in order to help patients experience how they came to be the way they are, and to "work through" early disappointments and frustrations in the patient/therapist dyad. By having an ongoing experience where the analyst responds to the patient in ways that take the patient's nascent, developing self into account, the patient will be able to trust and depend on the analyst. Eventually, the patients will be able to give up their omnipotent defenses, and find real ways of engaging in the world—ways in which they can learn to accept being "ordinary," and even to be okay with that. Monique understood how Aden got to be the way he was, but I am not sure if she was able to put it plainly to Aden so he could really understand it. As a result, he and Monique got into a bit of a tangle, with her trying to persuade him to give up his defensive omnipotence.

Unknown Self/Foreign Other

Throughout our supervision, Monique and I considered the extent to which Aden's difficulties were impacted by his immigration experience, and how much his problems had to do with his defensive style. We brought our own distinct points of view to our understanding of his conflicts: Monique leaned toward applying psychoanalytic concepts to her understanding of the historical and sociocultural influences that organized his defenses, whereas my orientation provided me with a more psychoanalytically developmental point of view on defensive style. At the same time, my psychoanalytic training at the William Alanson White Institute had alerted me to some of the issues that come up when people immigrate, and I had thought a great deal about the role of self vs. other, being in vs. being out. Monique and I discussed our experiences of "otherness" and discovered that we each had much to learn from one another. Together, we read papers about race and otherness by Maurice Apprey and Howard Stein (1993), Kimberlyn Leary (1999), and Katherine Pogue White (2002) that I did not know, and that helped both of us to think more about Monique and her patient, and Monique and me. We also read Winnicott (1965) to deepen our understanding of the function of the false self in protecting the true self. Monique and I also talked about our own differences: my identity as a white American woman of privilege who had experienced developmental trauma and Monique's as a black American woman of African descent who understood the lasting impact of multigenerational traumas. Consequently, we both understood what it was like to feel like the "other" in the room, though for different reasons. Our discussions were frank and intense, and I believe that through hammering out our differences and disagreements, we achieved a level of intimacy, honesty, and genuine respect for one another.

In retrospect, the parallel process between my supervision of Monique and her therapy with Aden is striking to me. Monique and I worked out a model for mutuality. We each defended our own turf and yet when we fought with one another the result was one where we each beckoned the other toward clarity. We both insisted on being seen and treated by the other as subjects rather than as objects. By using the supervisory relationship to explore her thoughts and feelings, Monique was able to take this way of relating back to her patient. She was just simply able to "be" with Aden in the consulting room and that helped him to feel seen and known in a real way. The differences between them grew to matter less and, in turn, Monique began to see him more fully and grew to have real empathy for him.

From my current vantage point, I can see that there are a few things I might do differently now as her supervisor. First, had I been more helpful to Monique about her experience of being pregnant, I believe she would have been better able to open up the therapeutic space with Aden when he learned that she knew she was pregnant from the start of the treatment. Instead, I was overly identified with Aden, and his experience of loss. Next, I may have encouraged Monique to tell Aden that even though he needed to retreat into fantasy when he was growing up, he could give it up now that the defense was no longer necessary. I used to believe that. However, now I have come to believe the old adage that the past is not even past. It is always with us.

Overall, I feel the case progressed as it needed to, and I do believe that Aden grew a great deal from being in treatment with a beginning therapist who was as thoughtful, dedicated, and talented as Monique. She ends her paper by stating, "despite the challenges, it was my honor to have had the opportunity to know, to treat, and to share in the development of this man. I will forever hold onto the space we created together—in my mind and in my heart" (p. 65). I feel the same way about Monique—it has been an honor and privilege for me to know this open, committed, talented woman—then and now.

Select Bibliography

Apprey, M. and Stein, H. F. (1993). *Intersubjectivity, Projective Identification, and Otherness*. Pittsburgh, PA: Duquesne University Press.

Beebe, B. and Lachmann, F. (2002). *Infant Research and Adult Treatment: Co-Constructing Interactions*. Hillsdale, NJ: Analytic Press.

Benjamin, J. (2004). Beyond doer and done to: An intersubjective view of thirdness. *Psychoanalytic Quarterly*, 73, 5–46.

Bollas, C. (1983). *The Shadow of the Object: Psychoanalysis of the Unthought Known*. New York: Columbia University Press.

Brandchaft, B. (1993). To free the spirit from its cell. In A. I. Goldberg (Ed.), *A Decade of Progress: Progress in Self-psychology*, Vol. 10, pp. 209–230. Hillsdale, NJ: Analytic Press.

Fairbairn, W. R. D. (1940). Schizoid factors in the personality. In *An Object Relations Theory of the Personality*. New York: Basic Books.

Freud, S. (1925). *Instincts and their Vicissitudes*. Standard Edition, Vol. 19, pp. 69–83.

Khan, M. M. R. (1960). Clinical aspects of the schizoid personality. *International Journal of Psychoanalysis*, 41, 430–436.

Khan, M. M. R. (1964). Ego distortion, cumulative trauma, and the role of reconstruction in the analytic situation. *International Journal of Psychoanalysis*, 45: 272–279.

Kohut, H. (1977). *The Analysis of the Self: A Systematic Approach to the Psychoanalytic Treatment of Narcissistic Personality Disorders*. New York: International Universities Press.

Leary, K. (1999). Passing, posing, and "keeping it real." *Constellations*, 6(1), 85–86.

Loewald, H. (1977). Primary process, secondary process and language. In *Papers on Psychoanalysis*, pp. 372–383. New Haven, CT: Yale University Press.

Mahler, M., Pine, F. and Bergman, A. (1975). *The Psychological Birth of the Human Infant: Symbiosis and Individuation*. New York: Basic Books.

Orange, D. M., Atwood, G. E. and Stolorow, R. D. (1997). *Working Intersubjectively: Contextualism in Psychoanalytic Practice*. Hillsdale, NJ and London: Analytic Press.

Stern, D. (1985). *The Interpersonal World of the Infant*. New York: Basic Books.

White, K. P. (2002). Surviving hating and being hated: Some personal thoughts about racism from a psychoanalytic perspective. *Contemporary Psychoanalysis*, 38: 4, 401–422.

Winnicott, D. W. (1965). Ego distortion in terms of true and false self. *The Maturational Process and the Facilitating Environment*. New York: International Universities Press.

Winnicott, D. W. (1969). The use of an object. *International Journal of Psychoanalysis*, 50, 711–716.

7

BUILDING SAFETY AND CONTAINMENT

Responding to Challenges to the Frame With Both Parent and Child

Jane Caflisch

"Will my mom have to pay for this?"

With five minutes to go, Thomas, whose excitement had been building to a higher and higher pitch, suddenly aimed the ball away from the basket and towards the clock on the wall, throwing with all his force. The glass face shattered.

I remember the two of us standing together looking at the shards on the ground and the naked clock-face, both frozen in place for a moment. It felt like a spell had been broken, and the safety of our playroom, which we had been working to build since our treatment began four months before, fell away to reveal a world of too-real danger. I remember he seemed both afraid and transfixed, staring at the glass like he wanted to touch it. Shaken, I told him we would need to finish our session in another room because we might hurt ourselves in there. As we left together, he asked me, "Will my mom have to pay for this?"

Referral

When Thomas first came to therapy at the clinic where I was in training, he was six years old. It was October, and he had recently started first grade. His guidance counselor had referred him for therapy because of his intense separation anxiety when he was parted from his mother, Ciara, during the school day, and his persistent worries that she was in danger and needed his protection.

A small boy with beautiful, delicate features, Thomas bore a close resemblance to his mother, which seemed to be a source of pride for them both. His voice had the soft edges of a young child, and he could seem achingly vulnerable from one moment to the next, though at other times he mimicked a young man's exaggerated swagger as though trying it on for size. After his parents' separation three years before, Thomas had lived with Ciara in a small apartment, with relatives often passing through to visit and offer support. Ciara sometimes referred to Thomas, jokingly, as "the man of the house," and he seemed to pick up on this role and to take it quite seriously.

Ciara had been diagnosed with multiple sclerosis during her pregnancy with Thomas, and had been in and out of the hospital over the years when her symptoms became acute. During Thomas' first year of life, she had a severe episode and was told by her doctor that she might die. While she had recovered temporarily, her illness was characterized by progressive relapses that worsened over time, and her strength and stature had also been deteriorating. In an early parent session, she showed me an old family photograph, wincing at the contrast between her full figure in the picture and her fragile, almost birdlike frame at the time of our meeting.

Although her health was relatively stable when she first brought Thomas to meet with me, Ciara explained that her symptoms came and went unpredictably, and that she often went through bouts of intense fatigue, numbness, and muscle stiffness that made it difficult for her to play with Thomas, make breakfast for him, or walk him to school. She described trying to fight through her pain and exhaustion as best she could in order to reassure Thomas that everything was fine. She did not want him to know she was sick, and had gone to great lengths trying to hide her illness from him, even at moments when, she acknowledged, he clearly knew something was very wrong. For the first three years of his life, when she needed to be hospitalized she told Thomas that she was going on vacation. As he got older, she did tell him she was going to the hospital "to feel better," but shared very limited information about her illness or prognosis, and asked other family members to do the same.

Since he first started daycare at age three, Thomas had struggled with separations from his mother, but his distress had been escalating as he tried to adjust to the longer hours of first grade. When Ciara dropped him off at school in the morning, he would cry and protest. Throughout the school day he often interrupted class to explain his worries to his teacher, expressing a fear that his mother was dying and that he needed to go home and protect her. In a poignant attempt to call up his mother's presence during periods of separation, he had begun signing his assignments with both their names, and including a depiction of her in any drawings he made. When these attempts to regulate his anxiety failed, he would engage in increasingly disruptive behavior, walking out of class, yelling, or rolling on the classroom floor until his teacher called Ciara to take him home.

Over time, school staff began to suspect that, rather than helping reduce Thomas' disruptions, sending him home was increasing these behaviors, since he had learned that this was a reliable way to be reunited with his mother. They also expressed concern that Ciara's attempts to hide her illness from Thomas, while meant to protect him, were actually exacerbating his anxiety, as he could tell something was wrong but had no way of understanding what it was. They hoped that therapy might help with his separation anxiety, and also help him feel less overwhelmed by the shifts in his mother's illness.

Start of Treatment

When I first met Ciara, I was incredibly moved by her. As we spoke behind the one-way mirror during our initial interview, I remember experiencing her as vulnerable yet poised, graceful, and full of a quiet dignity. While I didn't see it this way at the time, I idealized her. In my mind, she was at the center of this story, a suffering, all-good mother trying to protect herself and her child from the cruel, faceless aggressor that was her illness. I remember leaving our first session unnerved by her illness' unpredictability, imagining, based on her description, that she could die at any moment. Over time, I would learn that this was Thomas' image of her as well, or at least one side of it.

This sense of urgency remained throughout the treatment. But as I will describe, as my relationship with Thomas grew and I learned more about his experience as well as hers, my idealized image of Ciara gave way, over time, to a more nuanced view. As these shifts took place, I sometimes struggled to navigate between my alliances to both mother and child, especially when these alliances felt at odds with each other. This balance felt especially challenging to negotiate as a clinician in training, disoriented as I often was by my own uncertainty about "what was really going on": in Thomas' mind, in Ciara's mind and body, in their relationship and in our relationship, as well as in my own emotions as I responded to them.

In many ways, this uncertainty mirrored Thomas' and Ciara's daily experience. Often it felt as though the three of us were all lost together, not knowing what might come next. I was able to use this experience to connect emotionally with both mother and son, and yet I also hoped our treatment could help build a scaffold for them to hold onto in the midst of all this uncertainty. These efforts on my part frequently fell through, however, and in this chapter I will try to make sense of why this may have been the case.

One challenge we faced from the beginning was the fact that so much between the three of us remained unspoken, especially around Ciara's illness. Like her family members, I had been instructed not to acknowledge her illness to Thomas in any but the vaguest of terms. It was a secret that filled the room. He and I could explore his fantasies about it through play, and we did so vividly. But to name it, and to place it in a context that might make it more understandable to him, was something only Ciara could do. I will describe our process around this dilemma, the ways I tried to approach it, and the consequences that followed, further below.

As I got to know Thomas through Ciara's descriptions and through our play sessions, I began to see evidence for the link his teachers had suggested between his anxiety and his limited understanding of her illness. In our playroom, he was hypervigilant, seeing signs of unpredictable danger everywhere. For example, in our first session he picked up a toy plane and, noticing an almost imperceptible speck of red on it, said, "There's blood. The people died." This narrative of sudden death—with Thomas shifting rapidly between the roles of witness, victim and aggressor—was a constant in almost every session afterwards. It became its own kind of predictability, which could be painful to witness, both as observer and participant. I remember sometimes wondering what use it was for us to play out this scenario again and again, wishing I could reassure him or help shift the repetitive narrative into a story with more possibilities. At the same time, I remember feeling it was important that his story, and the emotion behind it, be something I could hear and share with him, since to try to change it before we understood it together might leave him feeling even more alone.

In a Play-Doh® self-portrait that he made a few months later, Thomas created a visual image of his hypervigilance, depicting himself as a small, red person with large, pointed ears (he called them "bunny ears") protruding from his head. Afterwards I sometimes thought of him this way: always on alert, listening for warning signs that might be inaudible to others. Foreshadowing a theme that would emerge around his sense of twinship with Ciara, he also made a nearly identical figure to represent his mother, distinguishing them only by giving her a much larger head. Among other things, I understood this as representing his preoccupation with what might be going on not only in her body but also in her mind, both of which filled his field of vision yet were often obscure to him.

At home, Ciara said that Thomas was intensely attuned to shifts in her behavior and her ability to attend to him, and became worried and solicitous when she seemed weak or in pain. He tried to help her around the house, offered her cookies and juice as she lay in bed, and constantly asked if she was okay. On days when she seemed stronger, he was calmer at school, but on days when she seemed weaker, even when the change was slight, he would tell his teachers he thought she was dying.

With little information about the cause of these shifts in her, he tried to make sense of them as best he could, and often this seemed to involve searching for a cause within himself. Based on his behavior in sessions, I began to suspect that Thomas imagined—as children often do in the face of inexplicable events affecting those they love—that it was he who had damaged her, and only he who could heal her (e.g. Klein, 1937).

I saw this dynamic in our early sessions when, after becoming angry or destructive in the context of his play, Thomas often needed me to take him out to the waiting room to check on his mother and be sure she was alright. In those moments it felt as though the distance between his mother's body and the contents of his mind had collapsed, and he experienced his strong feelings—which came and went suddenly, like storms—as concretely dangerous. Once he had seen her, he could return to playing calmly for a while, reassured that she had not been harmed by his aggression. But his fear of the power his actions and emotions might hold over her was never far away. His question "will my mom have to pay for this?" after breaking our clock, while I heard it literally at first, echoed afterwards with this anxiety that she would have to suffer for what he felt and did.

A few months into treatment, Thomas' need to physically check on his mother decreased, but he began to act out dramatic shifts between excited aggression and sudden vulnerability that I understood as reflecting a similar dynamic. Usually while shooting baskets or playing another competitive game with me, he would get more and more worked up the more he succeeded, warning me gleefully, "If I get one more basket, I'm gonna explode! So you better cross your fingers, better cross your fingers so I don't shoot . . . " On cue, I would play the role of the worried onlooker, expressing my anxiety about this upcoming explosion, while also trying to mirror his excitement and wondering aloud what these "exploding-feelings" felt like inside his mind. When he made the basket, he would "explode" as promised, yelling, jumping and stomping wildly around the room. Often this cycle would repeat, with Thomas pausing to catch his breath and then resuming his "attack."

Yet when his excitement reached a certain pitch, all of a sudden he would collapse, lying stiff and motionless on the ground. The contrast was always startling. He seemed to be playing dead. When he was in this state, he would not speak at all for minutes at a time, and when he did he would speak in a soft, plaintive voice, asking me to bring him things or to tend to him.

The first few times this happened, my immediate reaction was to feel frightened that Thomas had hurt himself in the midst of his "explosion," and to try increasingly anxiously to get him to respond. Once I saw that he was not physically hurt, however, I realized that my initial panic may have echoed what Thomas felt when his mother suddenly became weak and unresponsive. As he lay still, I would sit with him and, using my own experience of what was going on between us, would try to express what it felt like to be with a person who shifted unpredictably from strength to weakness, presence to absence. I didn't expect him to respond, and I didn't make the link with his mother explicit, but I hoped my affect and descriptions might serve as a useful mirror for his own mind.

In these sudden shifts I could see the split between the powerful and vulnerable parts of Thomas, and how hard it was for him to experience these as integrated or to regulate the strong emotions each state evoked. As I commented to him during one of these sessions, sometimes it seemed like the only way for him to calm down was to "explode" and then collapse.

Beyond this, however, I also began to see these shifts as representing Thomas' attempt to merge with his mother, after moments of aggression, by identifying with her illness and fragility. Now he did not need to check on her in the waiting room, he could become her. Like signing his papers with both their names or including her in all his drawings, as he did at school, twinning with Ciara was a way of trying to reunite with her when they were separated, or when he feared for her safety. But the fantasy that seemed to underlie this identification was still that his aggression, or even simply his excitement if not kept under control, could harm her—and, by extension, him as well.

Creating Safety

As we observed these dynamics, one of the primary goals my supervisor and I set for Thomas' treatment was to help him experience his emotions as just that: emotions, powerfully felt, but belonging to his own mind rather than to concrete reality. I hoped we could work towards this goal through play, opening up more space for him to express his emotional experience symbolically.

As a beginning therapist just starting to work with children, I remember this goal seemed elegant and intuitive to me at first, but proved much messier and more challenging in practice. For Thomas, our play-space was fragile, and could suddenly collapse into a sense of literal threat or danger. I imagined the same might be true of his attempts to play with his mother, who was sometimes available to him as a "subjective object" (Winnicott, 1971) but could shift quickly back into the realm of physical bodies with their all-too-real vulnerability. Trying to understand his experience, I remember reading and thinking a lot about the ways symbolic space can break down in the face of illness and trauma. I also returned often to a paper by one of my professors at the time, Arietta Slade (1994), which suggested that, while symbolic play might be the starting-point for some child treatments, in other treatments the task of therapy is to help the child feel safe enough to be able to play in the first place.

How could I help to build this sense of safety, when so much of Thomas' experience—both of the external world and of his own emotions—felt unpredictable and overwhelming? And what did "safety" mean when the threat of his mother's illness was not in the past, but was continually present, an ongoing part of his daily life?

One way I had tried to create safety from the beginning of our work together was by setting up the frame of the treatment in a way that Thomas could rely on as containing and predictable. We would meet each week, at the same time, in the same room, and Ciara and I would meet every other week for parent sessions. While the objects in the room were shared with other children and therapists at the clinic, I would bring a special box each time that was just for Thomas and me, holding toys we used together and artwork he had made. We would use our sessions as a time for open expression, but would agree to three rules for safety: that we would not hurt ourselves, each other, or anything in the playroom on purpose (Tuber, 2008). Thomas readily agreed to these rules, and Ciara agreed to bring him regularly at our scheduled times.

Later in the treatment, another way I tried to create safety was by attempting to facilitate more open communication between Thomas and Ciara about her illness, hoping this might help contain his anxiety both about her wellbeing and about the power of his own emotions to affect her health.

In practice, however, each of these goals proved challenging to maintain. I will describe these challenges in greater detail below.

Time and Separation

One of the first challenges we encountered surrounded the predictability of our session times. While her intentions were to bring Thomas regularly, Ciara often called to cancel less than an hour in advance, sometimes because of her health but often for logistical reasons or other conflicts. Because of these cancelations, Thomas and I could sometimes go for long stretches between sessions, without having an opportunity to anticipate and prepare together for these breaks in advance.

When an unplanned break like this had happened, I could see his anxiety spike in our sessions afterwards, and could feel him struggling to decide whether to risk connecting with me again or to keep a safe distance. He became preoccupied with the time, repeatedly asking me, "How many minutes? How many minutes do we have now?" turning this into a kind of countdown. When we made drawings of ourselves one day, his comment about mine was, "That looks like you, but you forgot your watch!" I also noticed that after an unplanned separation, his play seemed more repetitive, and even more intensely focused on themes of death and danger. In these sessions, he often shifted from anxiety to an increasingly excited identification with the aggressor, and then back to anxiety as the end of the session approached and he anticipated reuniting with his mother.

For example, in our first session after an unplanned three-week break (the longest in the treatment), Thomas played out a repetitive scenario in which two characters, significantly named "the mother" and "the killer," along with a number of animals he crammed into the backseat of their car, drove off a cliff. Each time, Thomas would yell excitedly, "Who survived?!" He and I would then survey the wreckage, and in a coolly dispassionate voice he would declare that all of them had died. He wanted to replay this again and again, as though he were trying to master something, but it felt static, stuck in an endless loop.

In the moment it seemed he was both acting out his aggression towards his mother, perhaps partly around our separation, and at the same time expressing his fears of how she could be harmed. As was often the case in sessions like this, however, his fear was mostly disowned. In this context, I wondered how to respond to his excitement at the characters being in mortal danger, knowing it was only one side of the story. Should I simply stay with his affect and reflect back what he seemed to be experiencing, expressing curiosity about what was going on inside his mind? Should I try to shift the repetitive play in some way, and if so, how? In this session, as in many others, I often became the voice of fear, saying "Oh no!" as terrible events befell the characters in our play. But by taking this stance, I seemed to fuel Thomas' excitement even more.

Who was "the killer," I wondered? Was it Thomas? Ciara's illness? Some blend of the two? Near the end of the session, after asking me how much time we had left and realizing he would see his mother again soon, Thomas revealed that the killer was me. Picking up a toy telephone, he cried out softly, "Mom-my, come!" Then, as he held the receiver, we had the following exchange:

P: (Whispers to me) How many minutes do we have?

T: (I whisper back) Two and a half.

P: What do you mean only two and a half?

T: I know it's hard to say goodbye, Thomas, especially since we hadn't seen each other for such a long time before today.

P: (Whispers into the toy phone to "mother" so I can't hear him, then yells into the receiver) Okay, O-KAY! (Hangs up phone, then picks it up again) I'm calling 911.

T: Calling 911!

P: On you! I'm calling 911 on you.

T: On me! Oh no, what are you gonna report me for?

P: You killed somebody.

T: I killed somebody? Oh no—I know those people got killed, but I didn't realize it was me who killed them! Could I really have killed them without meaning to? (At this moment I was trying to speak to Thomas' fantasy that he might harm others through his emotions, though in retrospect I'm not sure whether this is actually what was on his mind.)

P: Hello, 911, somebody just killed somebody. Track them down and kill them.

T: Oh no, Thomas, I'm really scared now! I didn't think I hurt anyone, but now it seems like I'm gonna get hurt.

P: Yup (smiles).

T: Huh—you don't seem that worried about that, you actually seem a little happy about it!

P: Mm-hmm (smiles)! You're dead now.

T: (I gasp and slump down into my chair.)

P: Wake up. (I sit up) Dead? (I slump down) Up. Up. Dead. Dead. (Yells) Ayooooo! How many minutes? One more minute? (It seems the meaning of his "countdown" has shifted, and it's ambiguous whether he is asking about the time because he wants to stay, or because he wants to leave.)

T: One more minute.

P: Darn it.

T: Hmm. When we start talking about those people-getting-killed feelings it gets kind of exciting, but then it makes you want to go see your mom.

P: How many minutes now?

T: We've got . . . thirty seconds!

P: (Yells) What?!

T: We've got thirty more seconds.

P: (Starts counting down) One, two, three . . .

T: We're counting down?

P: (Nods, and keeps counting. I join him, and we count down together.) Four, five, six, seven, eight . . . (We count down to thirty.)

T: Alright, it's time to go. It's good to see you again, Thomas. A lot of feelings came up in our play today. We can think about them together some more next time. (I want him to know he hasn't actually hurt me, and that we can still stay connected. We walk out together.)

Thinking about this emotionally dense exchange afterwards, I realized that condemning me as "the killer" served, at least in part, as a way for Thomas to undo the aggression of the repetitive car-crashes, leaving his destructive feelings behind in our playroom before reuniting with Ciara. By projecting his aggression onto me, both he and his mother could remain safe and good.

While this dynamic likely would have emerged in our work regardless of the breaks in treatment, I did worry that he needed to rely more and more on projection, denial and undoing as defenses because of these unpredictable separations. Since he could never entirely trust when we would see each other again, he could not leave our play scenarios—and the emotions they evoked—unresolved, instead needing to close them abruptly before he left.

Thomas' reliance on denial in the face of separation came up especially poignantly in another session, this time defending against closeness and dependency. Acting out a dynamic described above, he had been shifting between aggressive excitement and lying stiffly on the ground, without speaking. Then, opening his eyes and looking at me intently for the first time in the session, Thomas asked in a soft, childlike voice, "Can you give me something to lay my head on? Like a bunny." I found a polar bear stuffed animal he had picked up earlier and offered it to him, and Thomas smiled and placed it under his head like a pillow. As I sat with him, he took the polar bear in his arms and cradled it, asking, "Can I have this?"

T: You want to take him home? (Thomas nods, caressing polar bear; his face is very gentle.) Mmm, soft. (Pause; Thomas caresses bear) That feels good to hold. (Pause; Thomas continues holding bear) You know, I can't let you leave with him, Thomas, but I can promise you he'll be here whenever we play together. I'm sorry. (Pause; Thomas cradles bear and strokes his head) Do you have any soft things like him at home? (Long pause; Thomas continues holding bear, and lies quietly on the ground.) Holding that soft bear just makes you want to be quiet.

P: (Long pause; holding bear. Then, shifting abruptly into an angry voice, he says) No, I do not have a soft thing like this at home.

T: You don't. (Thomas shakes head "no.") Did you used to when you were little?

P: Yes.

T: When did you stop having it?

P: When I was four.

T: When you were four? What happened to it?

P: (Quiet voice) My mom threw it.

T: Your mom threw it away? Oh no! I wonder what that felt like, losing your soft friend.

P: Kinda happy. (Flat voice; his "manic defense" isn't working very well here.)

T: Happy how?

P: Sad way.

T: Happy in a sad way?

P: Yeah.

T: Hmm. What does that mean, happy in a sad way?

P: (Pause) I had it since I was a baby.

T: So it was your friend for a long time (pause). Why'd your mom throw it away?

P: I don't know. Ask her that! I think she said it was dirty. Maybe it had sick.

At this moment I had a strong association to the children's book *The Velveteen Rabbit* (Brown, 1922), in which the child's toy rabbit, after having stayed by his side through his bout of scarlet fever, is thrown away because of its exposure to illness. His parents see it as contaminated, and "shabby" anyway, easily replaced by a new and shinier toy. The boy mourns the loss of his transitional object, however, knowing it cannot be replaced. While they are separated, we learn that the rabbit has become "Real" because of the boy's love.

In Thomas' memory of his transitional object from early childhood, contamination also seems to have been the cause for its loss. Yet the source and danger of this contamination remained vague and diffuse. Did it "have sick" because it stood for Thomas' mother? Or did she fear its constant use by him had made it "dirty," and perhaps a threat to her health? I never asked Ciara about this, and wondered what the story was. But as Thomas told it, it struck me as deeply sad.

As the session continued, Thomas kept holding the polar bear, and eventually started having the polar bear "shoot baskets," positioning the ball between its paws. Playing this way, he asked me again if he could bring the bear home: "Just one day I keep him." I said I knew that would feel so good, but I couldn't let him leave with anything from the room, since other children needed to play with them as well. I promised the bear would be there next time, and could be his special toy when he came to the clinic. Thomas looked disappointed, and then, with the radar he seemed to have developed for the end of sessions, asked, "What time is it?"

T: I think it may be time to go soon, let's see. We have a couple minutes.

P: (Thomas's mood shifts suddenly, becoming harder. He starts shooting baskets aggressively, and when I'm not looking he "dunks" and slams the basket down, then throws the polar bear on the floor. Then with a serious voice, says) I do not like polar bears.

T: You do not like polar bears?

P: Actually, I don't like him.

T: You don't like him?

P: No.

T: Oh, Thomas (sad voice)! So you went from really liking him and wanting to take him home to not liking him at all. I wonder how that change happened inside your mind?

P: And I don't wanna take him home.

As we prepared to leave the room, Thomas, who in previous sessions had always asked me to tie his shoes for him, tucked his laces into his shoes instead and headed out the door without saying goodbye. I felt sad, for him and for me, and for his need to abruptly deny the connection between us, as well as to deny his longing for a transitional object. Yet I understood why he needed to do it. I had disappointed him, and beyond that, he couldn't truly rely on when he would next see me, or the bear he had befriended.

In my next parent session with Ciara, I brought up the idea of having a transitional object for Thomas at home, suggesting this might help him self-soothe when he was anxious, and could help with separations. She said he had plenty of toys, but often broke them. A soft toy seemed "babyish," but she might get one if he wanted. Thomas never mentioned this in our sessions afterwards, and for some reason I hesitated to ask about it. I think I feared that if he still had no "soft things" of his own, my asking might make him feel this loss more acutely or intensify his need to deny the loss, since he had no control over the situation. In retrospect, I wish I had asked him anyway, and wondered aloud with him about his experience of this wish. I did follow up with Ciara about the suggestion of a transitional object, but each time we discussed it she would agree vaguely without taking action. Eventually I let the topic drop. I didn't want her to feel criticized. At the same time, I worried I was letting Thomas down.

As we were discussing Thomas' ongoing difficulties around separation, I also spoke with Ciara about the importance, for Thomas, of being able to count on a regular schedule for our sessions. I tried to help consider other options for bringing him to treatment if she was not feeling well or had a conflict, for example asking her brother, who she was close to, or Thomas' father, who lived nearby and sometimes took him to school. She was open to these ideas but did not pursue them, and I often found myself feeling hesitant to press her about the absences.

This hesitance was likely a reaction, in part, to my own tentativeness as a beginning therapist, but it also reflected my position as someone without children speaking with a parent, and as someone in good health speaking with someone with a serious chronic illness. In each of these positions I experienced Ciara as simultaneously vulnerable and powerful, both of which gave me pause in my attempts to set limits with her around the frame.

Like Thomas, who shifted between displays of anger in the playroom and intense identification and solicitousness while in Ciara's presence, I also experienced a split in my reactions to Ciara when these frame issues arose. When she canceled with little notice for weeks at a time, or when I heard about her throwing away Thomas' transitional object, I felt frustrated and sometimes critical; but I quickly chastised myself for these reactions, thinking I had no right to judge unless I knew what it was like to experience the challenges she faced on a daily basis. It became increasingly difficult to determine, however, where empathy ended and an enactment began.

As the unplanned absences continued, I began to worry that our treatment might be recreating the very dynamics around unpredictable separation that were already fueling Thomas' separation anxiety. Over time, as the end of a session approached, both Thomas and I seemed increasingly unsure of whether we would in fact see each other next time, or whether it would be weeks until we met again. I tried to engage him around what this experience was like, so that we could at least name the feelings that came up around separation. But I worried that this uncertainty in our treatment, building on the uncertainty of his life with his mother, might exacerbate his symptoms. If that was the case, should I suggest ending the treatment if Ciara could not bring him regularly? Or was something better than nothing, and should we do our best with the time we had?

If this had been an adult treatment, I might have intervened sooner and more directly, sharing what I thought was being enacted and suggesting that we either agree to try to understand this dynamic together, or agree to end the treatment for the time being. With Thomas, however, this felt harder to do, since he was my primary patient but had no control over the cancelations.

If an enactment was happening, it was with Ciara, and at first I had little sense of what this might be about. Eventually I began to wonder whether, beyond the chronic unpredictability of her health and daily life, the cancelations might also reflect some ambivalence on Ciara's part about what it would mean for Thomas to become less intensely preoccupied with her, or to develop a strong attachment outside their relationship. His anxiety clearly concerned her, and I believed that she wanted to help him feel more at-ease. Yet his anxiety was also a bond between them that could be a comfort to her in the midst of her own fear and loneliness around her illness.

From the start of our parent sessions, I had tried to offer Ciara as much support as I could, and had also suggested that she might benefit from a treatment of her own given the many challenges she was facing. She tentatively agreed this would be helpful and accepted a referral, but never followed up. When I would check in with her about it she always cited time constraints, which I could understand given the competing demands on her time as a single mother. But as some of her conflicts around Thomas' symptoms and separation began to emerge, I wished there was more I could do to intervene. I found a therapist at our clinic who could meet with Ciara during Thomas' session time, and offered this as what I hoped might be a convenient solution, but she remained hesitant. In fact, as in our parent sessions we came closer to Ciara's own areas of conflict, she started to miss these sessions as well. I will describe these developments further below.

First, however, I would like to address issues of safety and containment in my work with Thomas, as these presented another central dilemma in the treatment.

Safety and Containment

In addition to challenges to the predictability I had tried to create through regular session times, challenges also emerged around the safety of our space within sessions. As noted above, Thomas had agreed to the three rules I had set for our work together, promising we would not hurt ourselves, each other, or anything in the room on purpose. He never hurt (or tried to hurt) himself or me, but, while I genuinely believed he was not doing so "on purpose," Thomas sometimes became so over-excited that he began to kick or throw things. The main target of his kicking was a large wood dollhouse on our playroom floor that, while symbolically meaningful, was physically quite sturdy and could withstand his attacks. Usually the objects he threw were also soft enough that they did no damage. But even a soft basketball, when thrown hard enough, could break glass, as we learned when he aimed at our wall clock.

That the clock would be an object of his aggression was full of significance. So much of his anxiety crystalized around the unpredictability of time and separation and how little control he had over either, as I have described. When the glass shattered, however, we were no longer in the world of symbolic meaning, we were in the world of literal danger. Aside from immediate safety concerns, I worried that being able to break things in our playroom would confirm Thomas' fears that his emotions were too powerful, and that he could do lasting damage to a space—our room or, in his imagination, his mother's body—that was supposed to be a sanctuary.

Especially as a beginning therapist, throughout the treatment I struggled to find a balance between expression and containment. I wanted to invite Thomas to freely voice his emotions, including his anger and destructiveness, through words, actions and play. Yet I also needed to keep him and our playroom safe from physical harm, as well as from the emotional consequences having the power to harm could bring.

Having begun, through early experiences in supervision and through my own treatment, to recognize some of my own tendencies to miss or shy away from aggression internally or in clinical material, I was particularly determined not to let this be a blind-spot in my work with Thomas. This was a topic of much reflection for me at the time, and I approached it earnestly, effortfully. In retrospect, however, this beginner's determination may actually have led me to "over-correct," and to hesitate to set limits around physical aggression when to do so would have been appropriate.

After Thomas broke our clock, I realized I had failed to keep him safe. I was shaken. I called my supervisor to let her know what had happened, then found a broom and a vacuum cleaner and spent the next hour going over our playroom again and again, taking all the toys out of their bins to brush them off and check for any loose shards, making sure the space was safe for other children to use. Ours was the last session of the day, and I remember losing track of time, seeing the sky darken outside the window. When I got home I was still on edge, and kept imagining a child getting hurt while playing in our room. I wrote an email to the clinic listserv alerting the other therapists who worked there to be careful when they were there the next day, even though I knew, rationally, that I had cleaned the room thoroughly. After hitting send, I remember feeling relieved that people would know to be cautious, and then—as the hours went by—feeling very exposed. This was a failure of containment, and now everyone had witnessed it.

In the days after this session, my supervisor and I considered how to engage with Thomas around what had happened, and how to reestablish a sense of safety. The destruction had scared both of us, and I needed to acknowledge this and to create space for us to talk, or play, about it together if he wanted to. I needed to set limits, but to do so in a way that he would experience not as punitive but as empathic and structuring. My supervisor suggested setting a temporary "no throwing" rule, including basketballs, for the next two months, hoping this might help cool down the temperature in the room and help Thomas find other ways of expressing himself when he was angry or excited. At first I was somewhat skeptical, as I had tried setting similar, though less strict, limits with Thomas for a while without success. I expected that he would protest or ignore this new rule, and feared a power-struggle or a rupture in our relationship.

To my surprise, however, when I suggested we take a break from throwing, Thomas agreed immediately, and actually seemed relieved. Before introducing the rule, I had said I thought breaking the clock had frightened him, and that I wanted him to know his emotions didn't need to be frightening. He visibly calmed down, and in the sessions that followed he was able to engage more consistently in symbolic play for the first time.

This is one of the clinical moments I have thought about most in the past several years of my training, not only in working with children but also in working with adults, and with primary process material more generally. When sitting, for example, with an adult in a state of paranoia or psychosis, or seized by a need to attack or devalue me, remembering this moment with Thomas has helped me recall the containing function of limits, essential for the safety of both parties. They, I and the physical container that surrounds us need to survive. Creating room to express the whole range of human emotions is one of our primary tasks as therapists, but being able to express aggression and destruction too powerfully, past play-mode into reality-mode—to the point that, literally or figuratively, the glass actually shatters—can be terrifying, and can confirm people's worst fears about themselves. When I remember Thomas' relief at our "no throwing" rule, it helps me consider when setting a limit would be the most empathic response, and the importance of focusing on how to do so without shutting down an important emotional communication.

"It's Either Him or My Health"

As I tried to create a greater sense of containment for Thomas within our sessions, I also wanted to help Ciara create a greater sense of containment for him at home. To do this, I felt it was important for them to be able to communicate more openly about her illness, as his uncertainty about this was causing him so much anxiety. Together with my supervisor, and in keeping with the concerns raised by his teacher and guidance counselor when they referred him for treatment, I saw facilitating this conversation as another goal of our work.

If I could help Ciara feel more comfortable speaking openly with Thomas about her illness, I hoped this might help him understand that it was something that occurred outside his control, and that his emotions did not have the power to harm her. I thought it might be containing for him to know that the illness had a name, that there were certain patterns to it that Ciara and her doctors were following, that she was getting regular treatment, that her daily symptoms did not mean she was dying, and that when he noticed shifts in her, they were caused by the illness and not by him.

I also thought he would benefit from understanding that her illness was not contagious, and that, while he was navigating perilous emotional territory, he was not in physical danger. He often seemed to experience the boundary between himself and his mother as porous, and sometimes this manifested as a fear that he was in danger of becoming ill as well. As described above, he would dramatically act out her vulnerability in sessions, lying motionless on the floor and needing me to tend to him. He would also describe theories about illness that suggested a similar sense of porousness, for example telling me, "Mommy caught sick, so now I have sick."

Sometimes I probably imagined, wishfully or naively, that this intervention would help more than it actually could. It would be very hard for a child to fully understand an illness like this, especially since, even for Ciara, it remained to a certain extent unknowable. And even if he did understand it, he would likely still imagine he had more power than he did to affect the outcome, and would still experience the boundaries between himself and his mother as blurred at times. But my supervisor and I both felt that if Ciara's illness could become something that could at least be spoken about between them, rather than a frightening secret that left him seeing danger everywhere, this might help to regulate his anxiety.

During parent sessions, I began to share my thoughts and observations about why communicating with Thomas in this way might be helpful, while also trying to follow Ciara's lead and to create space for her ambivalence. Ciara acknowledged that she had tried very hard for a long time to hide her illness from Thomas, and spoke about some of her motivations for doing this and her worries about how knowing the truth might affect him. Yet at least on the surface, she allied with the idea that increased communication should be a shared goal. When I suggested that perhaps we could have a family session together with Thomas to help her take the first step towards discussing her illness with him, she expressed appreciation for this idea, saying it had been challenging to have this conversation on her own but that it might be easier with the additional support. We set a date for one month later, in mid-May, planning to have three parent sessions beforehand in which we could discuss what she would like to say and how I could best support her.

After these dates were set, however, Ciara disappeared. She brought Thomas to a few more sessions, but missed her next few parent sessions, citing logistical conflicts. The date we had planned for our family session came and went, and weeks turned into months since I had last seen Thomas or heard from Ciara. Since there had been unplanned breaks in the treatment before, I kept his time open for the first month, and kept imagining the two of them might walk through the clinic door the following week. But when this did not happen, I eventually realized they would not be returning. Fitting with the themes of our work, it was an unplanned-for and unspoken ending.

As I tried to make sense of this abrupt termination, I started to reflect further on what hiding her illness from Thomas had meant to Ciara. What I had not fully acknowledged at the time, I realized, was the function that the vagueness surrounding her illness played within their dyad, and the loss that giving this up may have represented for her. In retrospect, not addressing the depth of this conflict directly may in fact have contributed to the end of our treatment.

I understood that Ciara's hesitance to speak with Thomas about her illness had many layers. At the most basic level, she wanted to protect him, and wasn't sure how much knowledge he could handle. This was the way she had described her motivations to me, and often this was where our dialogue about it had remained. Beyond this, I imagined that to name her illness might have made it feel more real to both of them, and that hiding it from Thomas may have been a way Ciara tried to protect herself from this reality as well. Perhaps she even feared that speaking about the illness might have demeaned her in Thomas' eyes, causing him to see her as damaged, as she sometimes saw herself. These layers felt harder to name together, but were often on my mind when we met.

At another level—one I never found words for in our parent sessions—I had always felt how strong of a bond Ciara's illness had forged between herself and her son, and wondered whether she might have worried that explaining the illness would loosen this bond. She had brought him to treatment to help him separate from her with less distress, and yet over time her ambivalence about this separation had also begun to emerge. Given her illness' unpredictability and the possibility that it could eventually be fatal, perhaps she had wanted to hold Thomas as close as she could and, unconsciously, keeping this secret had been a powerful way of doing so.

While she wanted to keep him close, however, there had also been moments when she experienced him as persecuting her, and even experienced him as in league with her illness. In one parent session several months into treatment, for example, expressing exasperation at his ongoing behavioral problems, she had told me, "A few months ago my M.S. was in remission, but now it's back because of him." Later she added, "I feel like it's either him or my health."

Looking back on this session I began to realize that, when she was feeling overwhelmed, on an unconscious level Ciara may actually have aligned with Thomas' fantasy that he had the power to harm or heal her through his actions and emotions. If that was the case, this may have been another source of her hesitance to speak with him openly about her illness' cause and prognosis.

Reflecting on this exchange with Ciara and on my own internal responses to it, I started to notice a difference in my experience of holding a child's ambivalence towards a parent, versus a parent's ambivalence towards a child. This difference likely affected how empathically I was able to respond to Ciara in her moments of anger or blame towards Thomas, and may have kept me from seeing and acknowledging their relationship in all its dimensions.

When Thomas kicked the wood dollhouse, or sent the figurine he had called "the mother" hurtling off a ledge, I could understand the aggression in these actions as one communication among many. It usually did not feel frightening to mirror or join him in his aggression, because his love was also so clearly visible. Having been a child myself, I could remember what it felt like to hate your parents fiercely but in passing, all the while feeling reassured by the steady hum of your love for them that remains, quietly, in the background.

Not yet a parent, however, I could not draw from personal experience to understand what it is like to go through moments when you hate your children. Drawing from the experience of family, friends and colleagues, as well as papers like Winnicott's "Hate in the counter-transference" (Winnicott, 1949), on an intellectual level of course I knew that both love and hate are an integral part of parental experience. Yet on an emotional level, I found it harder to imagine how these moments of hate might be balanced by love in the ongoing relationship between parent and child. I couldn't yet approach these feelings with the trust that comes from lived experience. They felt more potentially destructive, and I was much more anxious and hesitant in my attempts to hold them in mind and process them with Ciara.

Perhaps if I could have stayed for longer with her experience of blaming Thomas, I could have helped her integrate those feelings more authentically with her experience of loving and worrying for him. As it was, they seemed to remain relatively split-off, and were enacted rather than spoken. It was as though one part of Ciara was usually in the room with me, setting the date for our family meeting and thanking me for the support, while another part of her was leaving my calls unanswered. I wonder whether, if I had more directly invited the other part of her into our sessions, this story might have ended differently.

In retrospect, I think my biggest failing in this treatment may have been my failure to find a shared language with Ciara for this ambivalence, including the parts of it that made me uncomfortable, before suggesting an intervention that may have left her saying one thing and doing another. Since I thought of Thomas, not Ciara, as my primary patient, and since Ciara declined a referral for her own treatment, doing this work together would have been challenging. Our time was limited, and my alliances were divided. At the same time, the continuity of the treatment depended completely on my alliance with Ciara. Perhaps as these dynamics unfolded, it could have made sense to conceptualize the treatment, at least in part, as a dyadic treatment, with a focus on mentalization and parental reflective functioning (Slade, 1999). I hesitated to shift the focus in this way because I wanted to support Thomas' separation, but in order to separate he also needed a secure base (Mahler et al., 1975).

After the treatment ended, so many of these questions lingered, especially questions about how things might have turned out differently if I had been more experienced, more skilled, more able to walk this tight-rope between the needs of parent and child. We had worked together for one academic year, and I felt like my relationship with Thomas was just beginning. But our clock had stopped suddenly and without warning, and my image of him stayed frozen in time. For years afterwards, I often wondered how he was and how Ciara was, but assumed I would never know.

Epilogue

Five years after my last session with Thomas, I was eating lunch in a sunlit courtyard near the hospital where I worked. It was the beginning of spring, and I was lost in thought, gazing absently at the new grass. Then a woman's voice behind me said, "Jane?" I looked around and, to my complete surprise, saw Ciara.

She was smiling, and looked almost exactly the same as she had when we worked together, though at least in my mind she seemed stronger, healthier. We greeted each other warmly, and she told me that Thomas still asks about me. I remember wondering in the moment if that was actually true, finding it hard to imagine Thomas holding onto the memory of our treatment so many years later, but I appreciated it anyway. He was about to finish sixth grade, she said, and had been doing well at his new school. It was "strict" and "had a lot of structure," which she felt had been good for him. I thought of my own process around limits in our treatment, and wondered how Thomas might be experiencing this new setting.

We spoke briefly, and then I had to leave. We never acknowledged the way the treatment ended, the lack of a goodbye, and we didn't speak about her illness, but when we parted we wished each other well. I had a strong feeling, familiar from years before, that we were interacting on one level, and that there was so much left unspoken beneath. But it was moving to see her, and to imagine Thomas as his eleven-year-old self. He must have grown and changed so much since we last saw each other, and now here he was, on the verge of adolescence. As I walked away, I kept hoping that he had found some sense of safety and groundedness that would help him weather the storms of his growing-up, and that Ciara had as well.

Acknowledgements

All my thanks to Denise Hien, Steve Tuber, Arietta Slade and Stephen Anen, for shaping my development as a child therapist and for helping me to think through this case while it was unfolding and in retrospect, and also to Thomas and Ciara, for trusting me with their experience and with this challenging work.

References

Brown, M. W. (1922). *The Velveteen Rabbit*. New York: George Doran Company.

Klein, M. (1937). Love, guilt and reparation. In M. Klein, *Love, Guilt and Reparation and Other Works*, 1921–1945. New York: The Free Press.

Mahler, M., Pine, F., & Bergman, A. (1975). *The Psychological Birth of the Human Infant: Symbiosis and Individuation*. New York: Basic Books.

Slade, A. (1994). Making meaning and making believe: Their role in the clinical process. In A. Slade & D. Wolf (Eds.), *Children at Play: Clinical and Developmental Approaches to Meaning and Representation*. New York: Oxford University Press.

Slade, A. (1999). Representation, symbolization and affect regulation in the concomitant treatment of a mother and child: Attachment theory and child psychotherapy. *Psychoanalytic Inquiry*, 19, 797–830.

Tuber, S. (2008). Child Intake Class. Lecture conducted from City College of the City University of New York, New York, NY.

Winnicott, D. W. (1949). Hate in the counter-transference. *International Journal of Psycho-Analysis*, 30, 69–74.

Winnicott, D. W. (1971). *Playing and Reality*. New York: Routledge.

8

"FOLLOWING THE AFFECT"

How My First Child Patient Helped Teach Me to Listen and See

Jason Royal

I think back fondly on my first child case, but also wistfully. I hadn't expected the emotional chords that it would strike. Yet looking back, I wonder whether my private emotional experience was somehow linked to the blossoming of the play.

I worked with my first child patient, a five-year-old boy, during my second year of doctoral training in clinical psychology.[1] My program gave me a wonderful training. But it was housed in a building that represented the worst of 1980s architecture: a glass atrium here and there couldn't make up for scores of windowless rooms and cinderblock hallways. Yet in the rooms that had windows, especially those facing north, the light could be luminous and cool, and the view glorious, stretching over city rooftops all the way to the Bronx. One such room was the graduate student lounge. Here, between classes or patients, I often killed time sitting on comfy brown couches, confiding and commiserating with my fellow students.

One day, probably sleep deprived, I was talking to Becky, an advanced student by a couple of years, which then seemed eons. I mentioned that my child case had missed two sessions with no word from the mother, despite my messages. I was worried they weren't coming back. As if knowing the story, Becky said, "Yeah. Losing the first one is really hard." Our clinic worked with many kids whose families, for reasons economic and otherwise, struggled to bring them to therapy consistently. Sometimes the struggle was so great that they stopped coming altogether. Perhaps this was a rite of passage for many of us new therapists. I wondered whether the wisdom of experience would eventually make such experiences easier.

Going into my training, I had imagined working with adults. With my very challenging first adult case, started the prior spring and supervised by a wonderful analyst with a musical ear, I had been captivated by the rhythm of speaking and silence, out of which the therapeutic connection emerged. Yet such work assumed two adults, each in his or her own chair, talking. True, this included nonverbal nuances as well: tone, facial expression, body language, silence. Still, all of this I equated with the possibility of a shared understanding, an anchor of sorts. I now know things are not so neat and simple. But then, facing the beginning of child work, I realized I had no gut sense of how it would go. What would our shared understanding look and feel like? How would I know when it was happening? I was not one of the students in my program who knew, in their bones, that they wanted to work with children. I imagined they knew something that I didn't.

My Turn

Each Tuesday in the fall of my second year, my small student cohort would meet with our seasoned professor for training in child intake. Two hours for case assignments and presentations. Then two hours for interviews. Each of us would meet first with the parent, and then on a subsequent Tuesday, to have a first play session with the child, all observed by the rest of the class and professor from behind a two-way mirror.

There had been a lull in new child cases through early October. But one day, things picked up, and it was my turn. I was handed the one-page form child screening form. The child's name was "Santiago." He was a few weeks shy of five years old, but already in kindergarten at a local parochial school. The form also contained his mother's name: I'll call her Ms. H. Although Ms. H had called the clinic, the form noted that Santiago was referred by the director of his school. Under "presenting issue," the form stated that Santiago had "emotional problems," that he was "a little jealous" of his nine-month-old half-sister, and that he had trouble "focusing" and "staying still." In addition, the form indicated that Santiago had a difficult relationship with his father and their weekend visits. Although our group discussed ADHD, sibling rivalry, and tensions around child custody, there wasn't much to go on. I was sailing into unknown territory.

The next day, I dialed what looked to be a cell phone number. A woman with a Spanish accent answered, her voice cluttered by street noise. I introduced myself and said why I was calling. After a few beats, her tone brightened by recognition, Ms. H said, "Oh . . . uh, yes . . . hello . . ." She agreed to the conditions of the interview, and worked out an appointment for a Tuesday afternoon two weeks later.

When the day came, I met Ms. H in the waiting room. She looked around 30. Dressed in denim under a rain slicker (it was pouring that day), she had dark, gently wavy hair to her shoulders, deep brown eyes that showed spark and worry in equal measure, and a tentative yet genuine smile. There were circles under her eyes, but these only heightened a sense of determination about her. After some paperwork and reminding her of the observational aspect of the interview,

I walked her to the room where we would talk, a square room brightly lit, with a low table and chairs, surrounded by shelves stuffed with a colorful cacophony of toys, games, puzzles, and blocks.

Once we settled and I invited her to begin, Ms. H spoke in English that was difficult, but vivid and expressive. She was soon tearful and frustrated, at her wit's end, pouring forth in flooding detail about her son, his difficulties, but also the pain and trials of their lives, her anger at Santiago's father, and the fights with her current husband around disciplining Santiago. At times, her voice became louder, her words pressured. I was relieved that I could hold my ground psychologically. I was still an inexperienced interviewer, there was more than I could follow, and I worked hard to direct the interview, not to mention containing the added anxiety of being observed by my entire class and professor. I was frankly frazzled by the end. Yet Ms. H and I had started what seemed like a good rapport. Even so, my supervisor noted that I would have to take care in how much I allowed her to lean on me, given her palpable craving for support. Although I needed a good alliance with her, I was to be her son's therapist, and this would be a tricky balance to strike. I'm not sure that I was ever able to do this, try as I did. I eventually understood that Ms. H was probably privately wary of me as well, although not obviously at first.

Santiago's Troubles

The school had reported since pre-K that Santiago was distractible and restless. He also had a hard time getting along with other kids, especially around sharing. This year, things had gotten worse. His distractibility remained, but now he disturbed other children and would not do homework.[2] This was despite his mother's assertion that he was "very smart" and "knew all the answers." Even more worrisome, he was beginning to hit other children, apparently punishing them for perceived infractions. Moreover, when Santiago tried to play with other kids, they would often reject him. Angry, he would try to force them to play, leading to further rejection. Santiago wondered why they didn't like him.

At home, Santiago had become increasingly unruly as well, with tantrums and oppositional behavior and attitude. Most concerning, he was "jealous" of his nine-month-old sister, Ana, being both possessive and physically "rough," as well as covetous of the attention showered upon the "new baby." Ms. H was concerned for the baby's safety. Santiago was also coming into conflict with his new step-father, sparking fights between husband and wife.

Despite Ms. H's frustrations, she was deeply identified with Santiago, especially with his intelligence and his capacity for love. She enjoyed retreating home with Santiago and Ana, to watch movies or to play. She "loved to hug and kiss them." It pained her greatly when other children rejected Santiago. This love and identification existed side-by-side with Ms. H's acknowledgement that she hit Santiago out of frustration. It seemed she could be intense, angry, and punitive, despite her own wishes. Indeed, my first hour or so with her gave me a sense of her intensity. Yet I also found her sympathetic and compelling.

Santiago's Family and Development

Santiago's family life was complicated. His parents were both immigrants from different Latin American countries. Ms. H and Santiago's father had had a tumultuous relationship that ended because he adamantly did not want a child. The split-up began a difficult period for mother and son that lasted for about two years. Ms. H worked around the clock to establish a financially stable home for Santiago, eventually succeeding.

There were several factors in Santiago's development whose impact stood as a question mark in my mind. First, Ms. H had been severely depressed during her pregnancy and for Santiago's first months. Second, there had been a significant disruption in attachment for Santiago during this period: he had been sent abroad with relatives for several months during infancy. Finally, Santiago was confused about his position in his family and about who his father was. He had both a step-father and, to some degree, his biological father in the picture. However, Santiago insisted that his maternal grandfather was his father. He could not understand why his mother would call the other man, his actual father, his "pappy." ("Pappy is my pappy!" he would say, meaning his grandfather.)

Behind the Scenes

By this point, I was working with a supervisor, Dr. L. In her warm, low-keyed, sometimes wry manner, Dr. L began working with me around setting up the frame; beginning to intervene with the mother around parenting (e.g., avoiding hitting Santiago); and choosing materials for play with Santiago, which would form a play "kit" that Santiago would know was "ours" alone. (Santiago, when he understood, liked this very much.) She then mostly helped me to stay out of the way (!) of the unfolding of Santiago's play: learning to be with him in session, containing when necessary without directing. And most important, we talked about how I might voice what I saw and felt in the play. I also presented Santiago's play sessions in a practicum class, with Dr. T, where I gained useful insight, not only about this case, but also about what it means to "follow the affect" (a play session from this case, as well as some of the details of the supervision I received, appear in Tuber & Caflisch, 2011).

Still, I felt at loose ends on where to begin. The chaotic quality of Ms. H's story was striking, and she gave the sense that Santiago was out of control. I imagined trying to manage a Tasmanian devil of a child, pushing over stacks of toys, defiant and oppositional, and at best difficult to engage, even if I knew how. But beyond this, Santiago's difficulties reflected simply that he had been through a lot. This was going to be quite a ride, I thought.

First Contact with Santiago and First Play Narratives

I first saw Santiago on a school visit, prior to meeting him and introducing myself. School staff all commented on his distractibility and aggression. Yet I also noticed that they were fond of him, despite themselves. Why, if he was so difficult?

If I had to guess, it was because Santiago was exceptionally cute. He was slender and maybe a bit small for his age, with full dark-brown hair, pale-olive skin, and his mother's expressive dark brown eyes. He was bilingual, pronouncing English words with a lilting Spanish cadence. He was also a child whose penetrating look could suggest depths within, at times serious and melancholy. Santiago was endearing and, lucky for him, adults responded.

As I observed in class, Santiago would briefly attend to the lesson, but soon be off in his own world, looking around the room, thinking his thoughts to himself. He raised his hand to answer questions, but would forget the answer when called upon. But when Santiago got the teacher to come to him, he lit up with the engagement.

Sessions

Santiago was cooperative from the beginning of the first play session. At first, there were obsessional activities. Santiago noticed, for example, white pegs (the playing pieces of a game) littered around a playroom. He wanted to collect them. Or opening a new plastic bag of checker pieces, and wanting to get the pieces back into the snug but torn bag at the end of the session. And then there was his game of "smash!" Each of us, sitting opposite and apart on the floor, would propel our cars, blocks, or whatever, into the center of the room, smashing them together over and over. ("Let's play smash!") With board games, in which Santiago would make up the rules, and I would follow: he would want us to line up our playing pieces symmetrically, or to each take, say, two cards, which had to be "the same!"

Yet there were also episodes of what felt like primitive story play with animal and people figures, with a wooden dollhouse, and drawing with crayons and markers (we once made "aliens" from space). And of course, Play-Doh! But there were also eruptions of aggression that broke through the play, as in the vignette below, as well as "doldrums," times when I wondered whether we would ever stop aimlessly shuffling cards or arranging animal figures. Later, with Mousetrap, things would take off.

Santiago's Play: Vignettes

In one early session, Santiago goes to a toy chest and pulls out a hand puppet that looked like a policeman from the torso up. I pick out a "regular" man in a suit. I begin playing the character. "Hi, Mr. Policeman." "Hi, Mr. Man." "How are you today?" "I'm pretty good." "I'm pretty good too." But then, Santiago has the policemen exclaim, "I'm going to KILL you!" He then rams the police puppet's head into the stomach of my man puppet. "Ahhhhhhhh! Why are you killing me?" "Because you're the one who's getting me!" Santiago again rams the head of his puppet again into my puppet and I let me puppet drop to the floor . . . "Ahhh, you GOT me!"

Santiago laughs with glee. He then picks out a Lion puppet. I take a Zebra, and I begin for Mr. Zebra: "What's your name?" "I'm Mr. Lion." "Hi Mr. Lion, I'm Mr. Zebra." "Hello Mr. Zebra. How are you today?" Soon after, Santiago, using another puppet, says: "This is Mr. Bug." (pause) "Mr. Lion and Mr. Zebra have to EAT Mr. Bug!" "OK," I reply. Both of us make sounds of ferocious devouring as our puppets eat Mr. Bug: "Arrgh-arrgh-arrgh, arrgh-arrgh-arrgh!" When sated, Santiago has Mr. Lion make a loud "Burrpp!" Santiago then looks at me and Mr. Zebra, saying, "You have to burp, too!" As Mr. Zebra, I comply, with a low and gravelly "Bburrppp!" to Santiago's satisfaction.

Later, Mr. Bug is deemed "good" by Santiago, and therefore safe. But, we must eat "other bugs," otherwise know as wooden blocks. Santiago has Mr. Lion eat a bug, and then expels the bug from Mr. Lion's mouth onto the floor with a tremendous "burp!" I do the same. Mr. Lion and Mr. Zebra have a feeding frenzy on bugs, with ferocious growling sounds and burping. Santiago then decides that we must kill the "good" Mr. Bug after all. We slay Mr. Big, bashing him with our foam swords. Santiago stops, pleased. "We should play another game," he says. The feeling was that we were learning how to play "our" play. I simply followed, trying to play my part with feeling. My supervisor said this was just right.

Near the end, I say we'll have to stop soon. I suggest we clean up some toys. Santiago doesn't respond. His eyes wander around the room, settling on the foam swords. He walks over, picks them up, and hands one to me. He then raises his to duel. We begin. At first, he meets my sword with his, but soon he shifts to trying to "cut" me directly, aiming for my arms and stomach. The play intensifies. Although it still feels fun and playful, I also feel on the defensive. When he "gets" me, I say, "Oh! You GOT me!" and I keel over onto the floor. "Again!" he says.

We duel three more times. I then say, "OK, we can play more next week, when you come back." But Santiago continues to try to "get" me with an aggression that feels a little alarming. I say, "OK, let's stop." He keeps going with gusto. We've left the world of play. Unsure of what to do, I say, "You keep hitting me. You must be VERY mad." But this goes nowhere, so I say firmly, "OK, stop, stop, STOP." He stops and we look at each other.[3]

After a pause, I say, with what I hope is the right tone of calm authority, "Will you help me put away the toys?" He nods "no." "OK," I say, and I put away toys. "Let's go out to see what your mom is doing." Santiago says nothing, but smiles in a bemused way. As I finish up, Santiago spots a piece of

Play-Doh on the floor, picks it up, and goes to find the small plastic bin on the bookcase where it belongs. He pries open the bin, and looking in says, "It's all dry." He puts his piece in, and closes the bin.[4] Walking toward the waiting room, I see that Santiago is watching me, still with a vague, bemused smile on his face. He is trying to imitate my walk, following my rhythm and step. He seems excited.

Over a very few sessions, Santiago's play changed in character. What at first seemed like a "doldrum" game of Candyland turned into a rich reflection of Santiago's family constellation, except with me playing the excluded "orphan." Santiago begins by moving his piece all the way to:

S: . . . Candy Castle. I love Candy Castle!
J: You love Candy Castle?
S: Yes!
J: . . . Can I go all the way to Candy Castle, too?
S: You have to go to . . . HERE.
J: There? To Lord Licorice, at Licorice Castle? Hm. Doesn't look like it's as much fun . . . as Candy Castle. (Reluctantly) I wonder how I'm going to feel at Licorice Castle?

Here, I voice a question to elicit how Santiago wants me to feel. This came from supervision discussions of voicing affect in the play. Santiago, then pushes things along:

S: So go in!
J: Hm. OK. So now I'm in Licorice Castle.
S: Now I'm going to go in. (Santiago moves his piece into Candy Castle.) I'm in!
J: You're in Candy Castle!
S: I like this place because there's much fun.
J: There's much fun? Are you happy in Candy Castle? Hm. I'm not so sure I'm happy at Licorice Castle. It's kind of dark in here. And there are bats. (Dejected) Hm.

Later, Santiago declares:

S: OK. Now I'm going to go . . . to . . . (moves another of the pieces from the beginning of the trail) ALL the way to Candy Castle.
J: Candy Castle? Again? BOTH your guys get to be in Candy Castle?
S: Yes! And you only get to Licorice Castle.
J: I'm in Licorice Castle. (p) I'm not so happy about being in Licorice Castle. I don't think I like it so much. (p) Where does my second guy get to go?
S: Let me see. (S moves my "second-guy" piece . . .) You'll get to Candy Castle, too.

J: He gets to go to Candy Castle, too?

S: Yup. And he's SO alone (pointing to my piece at Licorice Castle)! With Licorice Man.

And then:

S: Are you going to cry?

J: Is he going to cry? I don't know.[5] He's feeling a little upset because he's stuck at Licorice Castle, and all of his friends are up here in Candy Castle.

S: Now he's getting away.

However, a momentary escape for Licorice Castle only goes from bad to worse:

J: What's going to happen? (voicing anxiety)

S: They're going to put him in jail, with the mud one.

J: Now he's in Gloppy.

S: Yesss . . . [6]

J: That seems worse that Licorice Castle.

S: Yesss . . .

J: Now how do you think he feels?

I'm not sure why I asked this, rather than playing "sad," but it drew something out:

S: Sad.

J: Sad? Is he stuck in Gloppy?

Santiago moves the piece to various places on the board.

J: He's all over the board.

S: He's sad.

J: He's sad everywhere.

S: He's sad. He's sad. He's sad. (moving the piece from place to place)

J: What's going on?

S: He can't go there (Candy Castle) because only THREE people can go there. And he gets in with him (Licorice Man).

J: He's back in Licorice Castle. So even though he tried to get away from Gloppy, he just ended up back in Licorice Castle. (Solemnly) Hmm.

S: Now I win.

J: You win?

S: You LOSE.

J: I lose?

S: Becaauuse — you do not know the answer!
J: The answer to what?

Santiago echoes further what's on his mind:

S: Tooo . . . (pause) Go over there! Just three persons!
J: Only three people can fit into Candy Castle?
S: Yeessss. (pause) I wonder what's in . . . I wonder what's in . . . his home?
J: I don't know. In Candy Castle, well . . . I bet there's candy in there.
S: In Licorice Castle . . . ?
J: In Licorice Castle there's just licorice and . . . well . . .
S: NOTHING else.
J: Nothing else. No candy there.

I note the powerful, punitive voice that Santiago uses to command me to remain alone, deprived of "candy" and having to witness others' bounty and happiness.

Signs of Progress and Otherwise

Santiago's play had begun to take shape. There were the superego-dominated voices, animal-oral need and aggression, and envy, projected onto me, of those who seemed to get all the love, all the "candy," that they wanted. And finally, most poignantly, was the sadness ("sad everywhere"), and Santiago's glee at finally not having to be the one who feels excluded, left to languish in an emotional Licorice Castle. (That role again fell to me!)

My play was taking shape as well. What I was discovering by working with Santiago was a part of myself that could both follow Santiago's lead but also be spontaneous: engaging with him through the characters in the play and giving voice to the current of his imagination and mine. Dr. L was encouraging, and I was having fun, even as it was hard work! And it was hard work. I was also recognizing that, since that first game of "smash," since the first time he said "yes" to "help" getting a toy off a shelf, Santiago had "gotten" to me. I think this had to do with being let into a little boy's imaginary world, slowly but surely.

Yet there were clouds already on the horizon. The fee, although low, was difficult for Ms. H to pay. I lowered it again. Also, she had gladly agreed to sessions twice per week, but as often as not, I saw him once per week. But added to these issues, Ms. H had learned that Santiago would not be "invited back" to his school for the fall. I worried that Ms. H's motivation for treatment was thinning.

These issues manifested themselves early in the treatment as cancellations and then "no shows." At first, Ms. H was avidly apologetic, but then perfunctory. Then she didn't call at all. (When I reached her, she said she had "forgotten," in a friendly but distracted tone, or didn't have her phone, or the clinic's number on her.) In person, Ms. H remained warm and congenial, although perhaps subtly less so. One day in January, she mentioned casually that she and her husband were thinking of moving the family to New Jersey "later in the spring," "maybe in June." My supervisor and I began to discuss how to encourage Ms. H to bring Santiago "consistently" until then. Even as my connection to Santiago had begun to sprout, the treatment felt precarious.

Play Session: The Discovery of Mousetrap

One day, Santiago and I use a new room, this one with windows, looking to the north, with the light and view I have described. After a few minutes noticing items in the room, excitement over new chalk, and drawing a snowflake on a blackboard, Santiago turns to the window, and says, "Look outside." We move to the window and look out. "It's still snowing outside," I say. To which Santiago replies with a quiet, even dreamy tone, "Yeah. That is my fa-vo-rite, fa-vo-rite thing." But soon, Santiago is struck by a board game:

S: OK, let's . . . what?!?
J: What are you looking at? (Santiago begins to pull the game Mousetrap from the windowsill.)
S: How you . . . how you call this game?
J: It's called Mousetrap.
S: Mousetrap?
J: I've never played it before.

After excitedly examining the many pieces, and figuring out how to put them together (he is pretty good at this), Santiago wants to get right to work, trapping mice!

S: Let's do it. Come on, do it!
J: Here we go.
S: Let's trap it now.(!!)
J: Trap it now? Doot doo-doot doo-doot, etc.[7] It's Mr. Mouse walking around. Oooh, I smell cheese! Look, there's cheese! Ooh, yum, yum, yum, etc. Ahhhhhh! (yelling with fright) I'm trapped! I'm trapped! I just wanted some cheese and now I'm trapped! I can't get out now.
S: (A kind of sinister laugh). He's trapped!

We continue trapping mice, but soon, Santiago wants to be the only one setting the traps:

S: Let me do it, let me do it!
J: Should I be the mouse? OK.

S: Doo doo doo doo doo! (My cue to be the mouse . . .)
J: I smell cheese. sniff, sniff, etc. (The mouse gasps.) Cheese! Mmmm . . . (but then) Ahhhh! (trapped)

Santiago is thrilled by trapping mice ("A-ha-ha!"). He cues me to begin another repetition in my role as a mouse. (Santiago is an expert "play" director):

S: He smells cheese.
J: (as mouse) I smell cheese somewhere. Where is it. Cheese. He's feeling nervous. He's afraid it's going to be a trap. But that cheese smells so good. (voicing conflict) He says, I'm going to get some cheese anyway. Even though it might be a trap, but mmmmmm. Ahhhhhh!

And again:

S: A-ha. Now it has to go like this. Da-da-da-da. Oh, cheese!
J: Oh, cheese! Yum-yum-yum . . .

Santiago enthusiastically insists on the mice's oral need:

S: Yum yum yum yum! You eat it!
J: Yum yum yum yum yum, etc. Ahhhhhh!

Soon, Santiago undoes the trapping, the set-up for more:

S: No more trap.
J: (as mouse) Yay! Now I can get out, and run away. It was really terrible being caught in that trap. I felt so scared. I was just eating cheese, and all of a sudden this trap came down. (talking to another mouse) Really, that must have been terrible. It's so hard when you're hungry all the time for cheese, and then these traps catch you. Yeah, I know.

Now he follows my lead and introduces more mice characters:

S: (Singing: two other mice come along . . .)
J: Hey look, there are two other mice. What are your names? You guys like to eat cheese, too?
S: Yes. Yes. (answering for the other two mice)
J: Have you ever gotten caught in a trap before?
S: No, we do not. (sic)
J: You've never been caught in a trap? Wow.
S: We do it like this. Dee, dee, dee, etc. When we smell cheese, we eat it too fast for the trap should not get us. (sic)

The mice eat and share cheese together. I have them notice the sound of a trap being set:

J: Hey, what's that sound?

But Santiago wants them completely unsuspecting:

S: Not! (sic) They're still eating.
J: Yum, yum, yum . . . Eating cheese, eating cheese. All sharing cheese, eating cheese (Santiago is preparing trap and then springs it on the mice, trapping them all) Ahhhhhh!

Santiago then brings in the "man" piece from Mousetrap who says, with a sinister laugh:

S: Bravo! Bravo!
J: Why is he saying bravo?
S: Because he gots all the mouse. (sic)
J: All in one trap!

He then starts one more repetition:

S: Now they're still safe (lifting trap). (as mouse) What was that?
J: I don't know what hit me. What happened?
S: They smell cheese, again! For everybody! (Santiago sets up several pieces of cheese.)
J: Cheese everywhere.
S: One, two, three, four (counting pieces of cheese)
J: There's enough cheese for all 4 of us, you guys! Come on over. We're so lucky to have found all this cheese. Very exciting.
S: (making eating noises)
J: Eating cheese, etc.
S: Ahhhhhhh! (traps one mouse, and then another)

For the mice, a horrific scene ensues. The mice are each knocked off, one by one, by frightening silver balls, twice the size of marbles, that Santiago brings out of nowhere:

J: Let's see if we can help him and get him out of the trap. Hurry, run. Run! Let's get away! (Santiago and the silver balls follow the mice.)
S: Ahh (another mouse gets it). Help him!
J: If we keep running in different directions, the balls won't be able to get us. (But Santiago chases them down.) Oh, no. Yellow mouse, he got hit. Ahh.

Red mouse got hit. Only two of them left, we have to get away. Blue mouse hit. Oh, blue mouse. Green mouse is the fastest one. He's going to try to get away. Where's he going to do. Oh, no . . .

But as it turns out, the mice's fate isn't decided yet. They now have to go to the "master":

S: (sinister laugh) Now the . . . the boss sends these guys to . . . the master.
J: The boss is sending them where?
S: To his master.
J: To his master . . . who's the master? Is this the master?
S: Yup!

Santiago almost slipped me here! But I was immediately intrigued by the enigmatic "master" figure, given his previous use of powerful, punitive voices:

J: So what's the master going to do with them? What's he going to say to them?
S: (as master) Put them there! (All the mice get put onto an "elevated" plank with a hole in it. Then, as falling mice) Ahhhh! (The mice fall, or are pushed, through a plank with a hole in it.)
J: They all have to fall through the hole, all the way down! Fall from so high up.

I don't know where this is going at this point. I'm just narrating what I see. Yet suddenly, Santiago wants me to take over as the master:

S: Thank you . . . (sinister) He says . . . (turning to me) he needs to say, "thank you" (gives me the master piece) . . .
J: (in a low "master" voice) Thank you, you silver mouse-eating balls. You did a fantastic job of getting those mice and bringing them up here so that I could throw them through the hole and they could fall down.
S: Boom! (falling sound)
J: Boom. . . . He must really hate mice.
S: He does hate mice.

Soon after Santiago loses the thread; perhaps there is too much aggression. The rest of the session is taken up with looking for and eventually finding (to Santiago's excitement) missing pieces of Mousetrap. But there are also moments when Santiago seems at a loose end, dumping out more toys and blocks, then ordering me to "clean these up!" We do end on a cooperative note, fitting pieces together, which engages Santiago. But I feel that there is more here for me to learn about helping him to modulate affect. Still, the play had taken on a new, enlivened, and elaborated quality. It was great fun.

Disappointment in the Waiting Room

At the following appointment, I met Santiago and his mother as usual, and he and I walked together to the playroom. But on this day, we weren't going to use the Mousetrap room. When we got to the room, Santiago looked in and refused to enter. When I said that we couldn't use "the other room" today, but that we could still play, Santiago looked at me, turned, and began walking back to the waiting room. When he got there, he sat by a little table with toys near his mother. As she understood what had happened, a look of frustration settled in her eyes. I had no idea how to handle this.

I told Ms. H that I would give Santiago a few minutes by himself. Just enough time, that is, to call Dr. L. I expected to get Dr. L's answering machine. How many New York City therapists pick up at midday? To my surprise and relief, she answered and I explained.

She said that I could still have the session. She instructed me to first try to talk to Santiago about his disappointment in not having the same room, and to say something about how hard it felt not to have our usual room. Part of my goal in this conversation was to communicate to Santiago that his disappointment was understandable and acceptable. I would not try to convince him to go to the play therapy room. However, the secondary goal was to model for his mother a response that was not punitive and focused on compliance.

Relieved to have the guidance, I said to Santiago, with mom nearby, "It's OK to be angry and disappointed. And it's OK if you stay here. I'm going to go to our room because it's our session time, and I'll be there thinking of you. But I'll come back and check on you to see how you're doing." Dr. L suggested that I have the entire session and, if necessary, allow Santiago to stay in the waiting room. He needed to know that I was "there," thinking of him, and that there was a place for all of his emotions. I went back to check on him at intervals, spending a few minutes each time. He never budged. At session's end, I confirmed our next appointment with Ms. H, who seemed fatigued and resigned. This episode reminded me of the fragility of our work. I wondered what Ms. H was thinking.

Mousetrap, Part 2

In the next session, following Dr. L's advice, I try to ask Santiago about the waiting-room incident: "You must have been very disappointed . . . " But he wouldn't engage with this. He did, however, engage immediately with Mousetrap: we were in the "good" room again. I would have to get us our own Mousetrap game to bring to any room.

The play continued with as much excitement as before. But now there were new characters, a mysterious Monkey and a Green Man. At one point, the evil

Green Man, who initially wants to trap the mice, is himself trapped. Santiago has him cry out for help. Although the mice know that the Green Man trapped them before, they are sympathetic and rescue him. But it's a trick.

J: Oh, so did the Green Man lure him in there?
S: He lure him! (sic)
J: He lured him in!
S: Now he's going to get the other ones! (evil laugh)
J: Ahhhhh! (mice panicking)

Eventually, though, Green Man is run over, by Barbie Corvette. The mice are, until that moment, about to walk the plank with the hole in it, jump in and drive off in the Corvette.

Here, I think the excitement becomes too much and there is no place left to go with it. This is another moment that I need to understand better. Santiago turns to other toys, dumping things out. He finds a play doctors kit:

S: Hmm! OK, now I'm the doctor. And this listens to your heart. (Santiago pulls out a toy stethoscope)
J: OK.
S: Now I'm going to listen to . . . (reaches to put stethoscope over my heart).
J: . . . You want to listen to my heart? Bump-bump, etc.
S: (laughs)
J: Did you hear something? (Santiago nods.)
S: OK. What is this for? (Pulling out a second toy stethoscope)
J: I think it's the same thing. So we both have them. You can listen to your heart and I can listen to my heart. Right? Bump-bump.
S: No! You listen to my heart, and I listen to your heart.
J: OK. (We put our stethoscopes over each other's hearts, and we each say "bump-bump, bump-bump, etc." Santiago laughs with glee. I smile.) That's pretty cool!
S: What is this for?
J: That is . . . that's for temperature. It's a thermometer.
S: For happy and sad?

We move on to puzzles and drawing with crayons, with a couple of attempts to go back to Mousetrap, but to no avail. At one point, Santiago is helping to pick up blocks and throwing them into their bin. He makes a long shot. We try to high-five, but miss:

S: Let's do it again.
J: OK. (We high-five again and don't quite get it, again)
S: We got it here . . . (Santiago points to his hand to show me that we were off-center . . .)

J: One more time. There. (I finish with the block bin, trying to clean up a bit, and then we high-five again, making a loud "slap!")

J: Yo!

S: Ahh-ha-ha-ha! We got it!

We end the session with Santiago coloring. He wants to try just "four more colors!"

Music From Within

When a child tells you he wants us to listen to each other's heartbeats with toy stethoscopes, and when he laughs with glee at the "boomp, boomp, boomp," he is telling you something loud and clear. I had wondered how I would know when some shared understanding was happening. Now I got it. But looking back, I can see that I had started to get it before I realized it. Following my own affect, I already sensed the new excitement of the first Mousetrap session. There was a freer, more elaborate cooperation in our play. We were taking cues from each other, and it seemed there was more "room" for both of us. Santiago's sense of excitement alone, along with his desire for repetition of trapping the mice and the pleasure he took in doing so, all of this said, "something is happening!"

I'm guessing Santiago felt it, too: a new safety and trust. Maybe that's why he was so disappointed when we couldn't go back to the same room after the first Mousetrap session. He wanted more of that, and was crestfallen just when he had started to hope for something reliable. Looking back on the ebb and flow of our previous sessions, from the obsessional defenses and games of "smash," to the cooperation, but with eruptions of superego-dominated control and more primitive oral need and aggression, I wonder whether all of this was his changing, complicated response to the anxiety of trust. But now it felt as if we had made the leap.

Here, too, is where the deepest chords were struck in me, the ones I had not expected. Coming from a primitive part of myself, perhaps the primal parent in me, I found myself feeling extraordinarily protective of him, and my own joy and excitement at the play was telling me clearly of my emotional investment in the work. The same message was contained within the emotional edge to my growing concern about the cancellations and no-shows. A connection was endangered.

I would clearly have to navigate all of this as the treatment continued. I cared very deeply about helping Santiago, but I was not his father, and I would need to take care of my countertransference both to Santiago, and to his mother, especially around her growing difficulties, both with coming to sessions and with protecting him generally from the turmoil of their lives. At the same time, I wonder in retrospect whether this emotional development in me was one of the conditions that Santiago, on some level, was looking for, as a sign that trusting would be safe. Maybe children have ears that are especially attuned to the moments when such low, emotional bell-tones, quiet and fathomless, are sounded within the adults around them, ringing with the desire to protect.

It is clear to me now that the deepening of trust and of the relationship were intertwined poignantly with the blossoming of the play. And after this particular session, I found myself feeling the lightness of a new optimism. Despite Santiago's problems, he could play creatively, and I felt the work had entered a new phase. I was also excited about what I would need to learn: how to contain and modulate Santiago's affect and excitement, especially when it became too much for him, which happened in this session, with Santiago coming to loose ends and needing to change activities. There were also issues of limit setting, and how much I should let him boss me around (usually around clean-up) vs. playing this role and voicing it as part of the work. There was also plenty of work to do with his mother. Dr. L was sure that Santiago could be helped a lot by consistent play therapy, even for a few months, and I was beginning to feel that myself.

Denouement

At the end of this second Mousetrap session, when Santiago has tried the fourth of his "four more colors," I say we need to stop and "go out to see what Mommy's doing." Santiago does what had become the usual: he goes right to the door, and then, looking back at me with his hand reaching up to the knob, he says, with play-provocative glee and a sparkle in his eye, "I'm going to turn off the lights, and leave you ALL alone!" I reply, in a play-scared voice, "But I'm a-fraid of the dark!" To which he replies, "I am going to leave you, and you are going to cry and cry!" With this, he opens the door, flicks the lights off, and is out in a flash.

I grab the keys and close up the room. When I turn the corner into the main hallway, Santiago is a few feet ahead, looking over his shoulder to see if I'm following. He calls out, "Try to catch me!" and then runs on his little legs down the hall, quiet and empty, with me trailing behind, seeing that he doesn't fall or otherwise get into trouble. We reach the end of the hallway, where he tries, with some success, to push open a heavy fire door that separates the hallway from the lobby area and waiting room. When I reach the door and help, he slips through and into the bright daylight of the waiting room a few feet away. As I follow him in, I see him leap into his mother's lap. Taken by surprise, she may have made a little "ooff" sound on impact, saying, with tired affection, "Oh, Santiago." As I approach to say hello to Ms. H, Santiago almost shouts, "Do you have any kids?" I say I don't. But he insists, "Yes you do! You have a boy and a girl!" I smile, not sure what to say. "Well, let's talk about it next time." I say goodbye to them, and add, looking back at him before exiting, "I'll see you next Tuesday, Santiago." I catch his eye and wave goodbye as I go.

But Tuesday never came. I never saw Santiago again.

Epilogue

The days after the missed session drifted by. I called to leave messages, but Ms. H didn't pick up and didn't call back. It slowly sank in that they were probably gone, after barely four months. I was feeling disappointed and angry at Santiago's mother. Yet I also knew that she was determined to make a better life for him, herself and her family. I imagined the therapy, which was difficult for her to maintain, no longer made sense to her. I wondered whether it ever did, once the initial crisis with the school passed. Maybe I could have done more about that. Aside from all of this, I did feel some relief, too. I had other patients, and huge amounts of work, the rich overload of my early graduate training. Yet I could still hear the dim ring of those chords. I missed Santiago, although I never said it in so many words.

I've had many patients since that first child case, and many supervisors. Soon I'll be practicing on my own. My technique and confidence as a therapist have grown in the intervening years, and that feels good. But one of the things I learned from Santiago was a special kind of willingness: to go with the winds and currents of the play, without insisting on knowing where. When safety and acceptance are givens, and when discovery and putting-into-words is the thera-peutic goal, then I think this special willingness on the therapist's part makes discovery possible for the patient, child or adult.

A few weeks after that last session, I met again with Dr. L. I mentioned that, per clinic policy, I would draft and send a closure letter to Ms. H. We discussed the contents of this letter. But then Dr. L said, "You should write a letter to Santiago, too." In the letter, she explained, I should say something along the lines that I was sorry we couldn't play together, but that I understood he wasn't able to come anymore. I could also let him know that I would remember our work, and I hoped he was doing OK.

I liked the idea. Yet I then began to wonder, would the letter get to him? Maybe they had moved. And even if it did, would his mother read it to him? Maybe something of my questions conveyed my lingering struggle with the end of this case. Dr. L thought for a minute. Finally she said, "I think all you can do is write the letter. And then you can send it to him," adding with a shrug, "And then after that . . . " She looked at me for a beat with quiet kindness. "And then . . . I think you're done."

Notes

1 This write-up is based on notes, written case reports, session transcripts, and memory. Patient and family names and other identifiers have been changed or omitted for confidentiality. Session excerpts have been edited for the purpose of this paper.
2 Without elaborating, I will at least note both my questions at the time about whether Santiago was old enough for kindergarten.
3 My supervisor suggested that I remind Santiago of the "rules" of our therapy: we can play anything, including play fighting, but we can't really try to hurt each other or

ourselves, or break anything in the room. These rules would also allow me to name and stop "not-play" aggression more, and to speak to it, more easily. However, such an episode never occurred again.

4 Perhaps he decided to help me after all. I wonder now whether this response was a positive one, related to how I handled his aggression (without scolding) a minute before.

5 Looking back from now, I see that my defenses come up in the play, too. Why wouldn't I "play-cry" when Santiago gave me the cue?

6 Imagine a five-year-old's version of a sinister voice speaking from the shadows.

7 My sing-song, skipping-rhythm words for "mice walking along minding their own business."

9

"PSYCHIC TWINS"

A Psycho-dynamically Informed Treatment of a Selectively Mute Adolescent and Her Mother

Zoë Berko

Introductory Comments

This chapter describes a year-long treatment with a selective mute (SM) adolescent whom I shall refer to as "J." I had never worked with any person with this symptom before. I thus found myself quickly driven to look to the clinical and empirical literature describing this syndrome to give me a chance to set my bearings somewhat. Despite long-standing recognition that the shaping and maintenance of selective mutism (SM) is embedded in family dynamics (e.g., Pustrom & Speers, 1964) with the frequent observation of a hostile, symbiotic tie to the mother (e.g., Browne, Wilson, & Laybourne, 1963; Hayden, 1981; Wright, 1968) I discovered that there are few published case studies that provide in-depth presentation and analysis of parental involvement in the treatment of selectively mute children either in the form of adjunctive parent work along-side individual therapy (e.g., Atoynatan, 1986; Inoa Vazquez & Myers, 2002) or family therapy (e.g., Tatem & Delcampo, 1995). Furthermore, the existing SM treatment literature from behavioral, psychodynamic and systemic perspectives focuses almost exclusively on preadolescent children, with a paucity of literature on adolescents despite the recognized difficulty of dislodging this symptom after a decade or more of existence (Hayden, 1981). This made my turning to the literature as a beginning therapist in search of guidance quite daunting. Indeed, I was able to locate only four case studies about the treatment of adolescents with SM (Jacobson, 1995; Kaplan & Escoll, 1973; Wassing, 1973; Youngerman, 1979). Only two of these cases involve childhood onset of the disorder that had persisted, as for J., into adolescence. Furthermore, they offered either minimal discussion of adjunctive home-based family therapy sessions (Youngerman, 1979) or entirely omitted discussion of parent work conducted by a second clinician despite acknowledgement that it constituted a "part of the integral treatment" (Wassing, 1973, p. 86). I thus found myself swimming in uncharted waters: how was I to be at all helpful to my patient given such scant training in this area?

My training in my doctoral program's clinic provided my first exposure to outpatient work with adolescents. Particularly formative was a two and one half year treatment of a female adolescent who presented with oppositional behavior in the context of an anaclitically oriented depression. The treatment included bi-weekly parent sessions with her mother. My work with this mother-daughter dyad, and in particular, weekly supervision over the course of the treatment, brought into sharp focus this dyad's struggles around the developmental tasks of separation and individuation and the reactivation of their struggles around autonomy and attachment in the transference and counter-transference dynamics of patient and parent work (Perl, 2008). I drew greatly on this supervision for my subsequent dyadic work with J. and her mother in their own reluctant navigation through the developmental process of separation and individuation towards a new relational configuration.

My doctoral coursework had included a two-semester course in infant and child socio-emotional development. Mahler's theory of separation and individuation (Mahler, Pine, & Bergman, 1975) presented in this course and more specifically, her writing on "panic tantrums" as dominating the clinical picture of symbiotic infantile psychosis would provide the lens through which I would come to conceptualize J.'s symptom picture. The completion of three sequential observations of a mother-infant/toddler dyad in this course along with a mother-infant therapy case during my internship, but perhaps primarily my own experience as the mother of a toddler, gave me a lived developmental context in which to place J. and her mother's unfolding interactions in the therapy room. In previous parent work as a non-parent, I had never entirely shaken off the feeling of being somewhat of an imposter. Now, and particularly with J. and her mother's initial relational dynamics reminiscent of the symbiotic dependency characteristic of early infancy that I had just recently traversed, I felt a much greater degree of comfort with parent work. My graduate training in family therapy also helped shape my systemic conceptualization of this case and certain of my interventions and I constantly tried to look at the case through both an individual and familial lens. It was thus with these aforementioned academic, clinical and personal experiences that I embarked upon my work with J. and her mother.

The Case of "J"

J., a sixteen-year-old third-generation immigrant of Anglo-Canadian heritage, was a selectively mute and school-refusing adolescent who was assigned to me as a transfer case during my internship. For the preceding seven months J. had inconsistently attended weekly (primarily behavioral) therapy with a pre-doctoral extern with regular separate parent sessions held with her mother who had recently been prevailed upon to allow J. to begin anxiolytic medication. Chart notes indicated that throughout the treatment, despite the offer of behavioral rewards, J. had exhibited considerable difficulties tolerating separation from her mother to meet alone with the therapist. She persistently refused to enter the therapy room, requiring her mother to accompany her and then remain in the room or within her line of vision though the open door. When separated from mother, J. exhibited regressed behavior such as lying on the floor of the therapy room. Despite some intermittent monosyllabic answers in response to the therapist's questions and some whispered speech with her mother in the therapist's presence over the course of the treatment, her SM had not (as during a prior treatment during early adolescence) abated.

J. and her mother arrived thirty minutes late to our first session and were seen jointly for the remaining fifteen minutes. J., a slimly built, physically underdeveloped teen who appeared markedly younger than her chronological age, entered the therapy room alongside her mother, avoiding eye contact with me. Striding deliberately towards the back of the elongated therapy room she selected a child's sized chair that she turned to face the wall. This would remain her preferred seat throughout our year-long treatment. The rigidity of her immobile, closed posture, her constricted affect and minimal non-verbal communication in response to my inquiries about her prior experience of treatment lent her a frozen yet seething air. Mother voiced her daughter's intense opposition, endorsed by J.'s vigorous head nod, to being in treatment and working towards the resolution of her mutism. I was intrigued by J.'s presentation and by the inner world that lay behind her silence.

Her mother, a visibly timid woman, took up a seat next to me as she apologized for their late arrival. "It feels like I have two daughters," she explained, describing her experience of her daughter's dual personalities; namely, the mute, clinging child-like public persona and the verbal, negativistic adolescent who re-emerged upon crossing the household threshold. At my invitation, she outlined J.'s interrelated history of selective mutism and school refusal behaviors (daily temper tantrums and frequent somatic concerns) that had intensified since their onset upon J.'s entry into kindergarten—her first separation from her nuclear family who remained the only people with whom she spoke aside from a younger teenaged friend from her old neighborhood.

The recommendation for family therapy was reiterated in light of J.'s continued struggle to tolerate separation from mother. The implications of her presentation for the family system, namely, the impending threat of the involvement of child protective services due to her school refusal, also weighed heavily on J.'s need for a more productive treatment. In addition, her parents' struggle to manage J.'s temper tantrums was exacerbated by their differing conceptualizations of this behavior as reflecting oppositional behavior (for father) or anxiety about school attendance (for mother). The next session mother confirmed (as she anticipated) father's continued refusal to participate in J.'s treatment at the next session. Over time, to my great frustration, I would come to view mother as a gatekeeper who thwarted my repeated efforts to engage J.'s father in the treatment.

Subsequent sessions that focused on identifying the factors that had shaped the origin and maintenance of these behaviors allowed me to place J.'s symptom picture in the following relational context: a closed and socially isolated family system with a difficult and often symbiotic mother-daughter relationship that largely excluded a seemingly passive and absent father with an overly sheltered sibling cast in the role of understudy should J. ever vacate her sick role. I came to picture the family hunkered down in the fortress of their apartment scurrying out only for essential supplies and medical treatment. The above-described familial characteristics are consistent with Hayden's (1981) description of symbiotic mutism, the most common of four types of selective mutism differentiated by Hayden (the others being passive-aggressive, reactive and speech phobic).

The Search for a Therapeutic Stance

With no prior clinical experience with SM and given the rarity of J.'s presentation, I turned to the psychodynamic and family systems case study literature at the outset of my work with J. and her mother for guidance on approaches to treatment to explore with my child therapy supervisor. Indeed, throughout the treatment I found myself repeatedly returning to the literature, consulting various supervisors at my internship site as well as my dissertation chair during academic advisement meetings. Retrospectively, I have come to view this repeated injection of the outside supervisory world into my supervisory dyad as perhaps also driven by the locked in quality of the patient-parent dyad and a need to expand my feelings of being implanted, via parallel process, within a closed and isolated family system.

In my literature search, I came across Crenshaw's (2007) paper about his treatment of a six-year-old girl with SM whose "coming to voice" was facilitated through play therapy involving games of hide and seek with puppets and adjunctive family sessions. Bringing this paper into supervision, my child supervisor and I pondered how this treatment modality could be adapted for an adolescent. I was as yet unsure if J. had attained the capacity to play (Winnicott, 1971) or whether she felt in some way prohibited from being playful in her mother's presence. We knew she would have to be engaged in a unique manner but at this juncture were unsure how. Furthermore, despite my realization that J.'s mutism was deeply entrenched and had not yielded to the efforts of two prior therapists, I felt a sense of urgency to effect behavioral change given the impending threat of the involvement of Child Protective Services. The time-limited nature of the treatment only exacerbated this sense of urgency, an urgency not matched by J.'s mother. Crenshaw's (2007) guidance to "dispense with all expectations that she would speak" but instead "just focus on being fully in the moment with her and see 'what-if' anything happens" (p. 20) tempered this sense of urgency and freed me to focus on the minute shifts of the unfolding treatment rather than feel defeated by her persistent silence. Crenshaw (2007) also cautioned against aligning oneself with adults who pressure the child to speak thereby heightening the child's anxiety and associated sense of power. His matter-of-fact comment on the eventual emergence of his patient's speech during a game of hide and seek ("it's my turn now") guided my own therapeutic stance and neutral response to J.'s gradual expanding non-verbal repertoire despite the inner exhilaration I felt in these moments.

Symbiotic Mutism: "Psychic Twins"

Mahler defines symbiosis as "a stage of sociobiological interdependence between the one to five month old infant and his mother, a stage of pre-object or need satisfying relationship in which self and maternal intra-psychic representations have not yet been differentiated" (Mahler et al., 1975, p. 290). During symbiosis, Mahler observes, the infant primarily invests his libidinal energy in his mother as opposed to the external "other-than-mother" world.

J. and her mother were initially seen dyadically given their symbiotic dependency, evidenced by J.'s inability to tolerate separation from her mother who in turn appeared threatened by the prospect of her daughter developing "other-than-mother" relationships. Despite reservations that dyadic sessions might serve to reinforce their mutual dependency, and thus J.'s mutism, I sensed the importance of not immediately moving to disturb the deeply rooted dynamics of their relationship but rather gradually interposed myself first as a physical and then a relational "other-than-mother" presence within their symbiotic world. My hope was that, once accepted into their world, I could, first, through the modeling of a self-reflective stance and, subsequently, through the enhancement of their own capacities for self-reflection, create a therapeutic space that would allow mother and daughter to contemplate their distinct inner experiences and needs (Tuber & Caflisch, 2011) and support a gradual loosening of their hostile, dependent tie, leading to J.'s eventual individuation. A treatment alliance "built on an agreement to make sense of feelings" (Tuber & Caflisch, 2011, p. 6) versus the pretense of collaborating on symptom removal would prove critical in facilitating their engagement in the treatment. The mandatory establishment of a treatment plan (listing the resolution of J.'s mutism as its primary goal) and its review each quarter thus felt like a jarring intrusion into the therapeutic space I sought to create. As mother dutifully signed, J. glared at me angrily from the back of the room refusing to sign as I worried that this had only further alienated J. before our work had begun.

Our early work in which mother was encouraged to mentalize J.'s inner experiences, namely to wonder about her feelings, what they felt like and where they came from (Tuber & Caflisch, 2011) felt remarkably similar to parent-infant psychotherapy (Lieberman, Silverman, & Pawl, 1999). However, in contrast to my concurrent treatment of a mother and her ten-month-old at my internship site,

I felt largely unseen by J. at this stage. With mother as her voice, J. slowly began to participate nonverbally in the treatment, shrugging her shoulders and nodding her head to endorse or refute the thoughts, feelings and beliefs attributed to her by her mother and wondered about by the therapist. With a vigorous nod of her head J. conveyed that she welcomed mother's acknowledged tendency to "take over" and act as her public "voice." Significantly, despite mother's voiced exasperation about J.'s mutism, at no point during the treatment did mother encourage J. to speak with me. Rather, her observation, "Well, J. just doesn't like to share anything personal" seemed to instruct J. that her inner life should remain sealed off. Her related comment, "J. thinks therapists are weird" typecast me in the uni-dimensional role played by each of J.'s successive therapists, thereby foreclosing the possibility that over time I could become "knowable enough" to be a new object that J. could put to use (Gaines, 2003, p. 576). This comment also highlighted for me the impossibility of disentangling mother and daughter's negative projections.

As summer drew to a close and school resumed, mother disclosed her intention to keep J. home from school for the foreseeable future, an arrangement that J. visibly approved. Defeated by years of daily battles to get J. to school, mother expressed her hope that this would finally force the Board of Education to initiate home instruction. Subsequent sessions focused on gently exploring the dyad's feelings about J. moving beyond the symbiotic orbit. With a mock weary sigh, mother proclaimed, "J. wants to stay with me forever." Mother expanded (and J. confirmed nonverbally) that J. did not wish to complete high school, enter the world of employment, live independently, marry or have children of her own. Rather, J. desired to stay home tending to her menagerie of pets.

Mother's continued definitive attributions of J.'s mental states felt reminiscent of Bateman and Fonagy's (2006) concept of intrusive pseudo-mentalization. This is noted to occur in the context of intense attachment relationships, and defined as "arise[ing] when the separateness or opaqueness of minds is not respected. The individuals believe they 'know' how or what another person feels or thinks" (Bateman & Fonagy, 2006, p. 73). Mother's intrusive pseudo-mentalization of J.'s emotions, beliefs and intentions was confirmed by her disclosure that she saw herself and her daughter as "psychic twins."

Mother's characterization of the dyad as "psychic twins" brought to mind my earlier reading of *The Silent Twins*, Wallace's (1986) book about the selectively mute Gibbons twins who during childhood retreat from their perceived hostile environment into an imaginary world of their own co-creation. Sacks (1986) draws on Burlingham's (1945) examination of the twin bond to illuminate his discussion of this case, specifically, the emergence of self-destructive and suicidal behavior in the Gibbons twins as they struggle to navigate the intensification of their struggles around separation and individuation during adolescence. Twins, Sacks (1986) notes, are generally able to achieve differentiation "while maintaining this singular tie" (p. 3). However, on occasions this tie may become pathological—Burlingham speaks here of the twin pair becoming a "twin-team" or "twin gang," feeling, doing everything together, caught in a helpless entanglement or embrace. Such an embrace—at once yearned for and intolerable—tends to be both symbiotic and destructive.

(Sacks, 1986, p. 3)

I began to wonder whether J. really wished to remain forever locked into this symbiotic fusion with her mother. If not, how and through what process could J. extricate herself from this relationship? With the dyad's unexpressed mutual hostility palpable in the therapy room, I braced myself for its emergence, worrying that their journey towards intra-psychic separation could only be realized through some degree of destruction of the self or other.

Our exploration of separation thus began on the safer, more distant terrain of the dyad's experience of separations during their respective early childhoods. Mother recounted her own considerable difficulty handling separations during early childhood requiring, as she recalled, her mother to remain at the back of her kindergarten class for the duration of the academic year. Her own history, she acknowledged, strengthened her identification with her daughter's struggles. Mother's experience of J.'s early autonomy strivings was a further focus of these sessions. Then, as throughout the first year of treatment, she struggled to access feelings of loss inherent in J.'s moves away from her towards independence. Rather, she stuck to the concrete drawbacks such as accidents associated with toilet training.

Emerging Differentiation

Mahler et al. (1975) define separation and individuation as follows:

[A] phase of development that lasts from about five months to two and half years, and moves along two separate but inter-twining tracks: the one of separation, leading to intrapsychic awareness of separateness, and the other of individuation, leading to the acquisition of a distinct and unique individuality.

(p. 292)

Differentiation (the first sub-phase of separation and individuation) is characterized by the infant's more permanent state of alertness coinciding with "the process of emerging from the symbiotic state of oneness with the mother, in the intra-psychic sense" (Mahler et al., 1975, p. 290). During this process, termed "hatching," the infant increasingly directs his perceptual attention to the external "other-than-mother" world. The beginning of J.'s occasional fleeting glances at me and her mother from the corner of the room felt reminiscent of Mahler's description of the infant's comparative scanning as I gradually came into view for her.

As our dyadic work continued to unfold, I began to gently highlight instances of their converging and diverging perspectives to underscore the separateness of their minds. This shift in technique (and the dyad's ability to survive contemplation of their distinct inner worlds within the therapeutic space) appeared to support mother's disclosure of J.'s desire for an identical twin or baby sister. We explored the meaning this fantasy held for J., who confirmed with a nod of her head that she imagined the presence of a new sibling—and the unspoken rekindling of mother's intimate connection with father—would draw mother's emotional focus away from her. This fantasy was paralleled by two further shifts: first, the gradual demarcation of her distinct physical presentation after months of J. and mother attending treatment similarly clad in items from their shared wardrobe; second, J.'s expression of support for the initiation of separate parent sessions reflecting her readiness for mother to build an independent relationship with the therapist.

Parent sessions with mother, initiated four months into the treatment, focused on exploring her intense anxiety about the wellbeing of her children outside of her presence, expressed in comments such as "kids get snatched from the streets all the time." My attempts to examine the reality basis of these fears were met with retorts such as, "girls go to college or away on spring break and get killed and those parents never thought it would happen to them" illustrating the difficulty of dislodging these distortions.

Winnicott (1958) defines the capacity to be alone as initially "the experience of being alone while someone else is present" (p. 417). For Winnicott, the capacity to be alone is rooted in the experience of being alone in the presence of the mother during infancy and early childhood. Thus, "an infant with weak ego organization may be alone because of the [mother's] reliable ego-support" (p. 419). Gradually, the child introjects the ego-supportive mother thereby developing the capacity to be alone "without frequent reference to the mother or mother symbol" (p. 418). For Winnicott, the development of the capacity to be alone is underpinned by "the existence in the psychic reality of the individual of a good object" and the related "belief in a benign environment" shaped by the experience of good-enough mothering, or as Winnicott puts it, "in negative terms, there must be a relative freedom from persecutory anxiety" (p. 417). Tethered to her mother's intergenerationally transmitted vision of the outside world as dangerous, J. could understandably not be alone in the presence of an "other-than-mother" figure. Rather, seemingly yet to achieve emotional object constancy, J. threw "panic tantrums" (Mahler et al., 1975) if mother did not remain within her line of vision when venturing outside the family's apartment.

This phase of the treatment was marked by the emergence of spontaneous non-verbal communication as J. banged her fist on the back of her chair to communicate her anger about mother's recently filed application for home instruction. Building upon our prior work about mother operating as J.'s public "voice," I shared my observation that I could well imagine the daunting prospect of negotiating social interactions in the absence of this voice. However, I was unable to elicit any form of non-verbal communication from J. to gauge the fit of my interpretation. Turning to mother, I shared my related observation of the imagined sense of desertion mother felt when unable to act as J.'s voice. Mother's quiet nod suggested that this resonated with her. After months of silent inertia, the vitality of J.'s rhythmic banging resounding around the room seemed to signal the gradual awakening of her desire for relatedness. Meeks and Bernet (2005) describe the conscious fear of "becoming embroiled in another dependency relationship" (p. 77) as a typical part of the therapeutic process with adolescent patients who are in the midst of disengaging from infantile objects in order to cathect new objects such as peers and, subsequently, romantic partners (Blos, 1967; A. Freud, 1958). I could only imagine that this fear was heightened for J., whose primary experience of relatedness was that of symbiotic dependency. Indeed, Hayden (1981) notes that symbiotic mutes in particular appear to "fear another entrapping relationship" (p. 121). As I had feared, J. retreated back into the symbiotic orbit as evidenced by the virtual shutdown of her non-verbal communication in the sessions that followed, reflecting her ambivalence around relating to an "other-than-mother-figure." Once again, I felt J. fade away in the room and mother resume her position of dominant presence and voice.

The Use of Photography to Facilitate "Coming to Voice"

Over the coming weeks, as J. resumed her restricted range of non-verbal communications (namely, head-nods and shakes, shoulder shrugs and banging), I began to reflect upon other non-verbal mediums to facilitate her "coming to voice." Previously, she had declined to draw, both within and outside of the sessions, despite the casualness with which I floated out this suggestion. Realizing the need to engage her in a unique way, I gave J. a disposable camera with the instruction to take some pictures "of things in your mother's world": thus worded (as guided by my therapy supervisor) to avoid a further defensive flight back into symbiosis. Mother scooped up the camera that I had placed within J.'s reach and placed it in her bag.

At the next session, mother described how "we" had worked on the photography assignment "together," again referencing J.'s reluctance to "share anything personal with you," due to her desire to "keep her life here and at home separate" so as "not to give up control over the situation." Once again, and with J. unwilling to own or refute these statements, I was unable to determine whose views they reflected but sensed mother's lead in selecting and controlling the images to be portrayed to the outside world. Subsequent sessions focused on exploring the meaning the photographs held for J. and her mother. The photos (all shot within the family's apartment) included numerous images of a smiling, relaxed J. with her pets as well as a few pictures of her sibling. Her father's absence was notable. I was left to wonder whether she would ever show me the private persona glimpsed in the photos. With the intimacy of her home-life exposed, J. pulled her chair behind my full-length winter coat that hung from the coat rail in the corner of the room and declined to participate in these next sessions. Indeed, with her face obscured from my view, her only response was to throw the pictures of her sibling on the floor, later communicating that this reflected anger about her sibling calling her "psycho" and "crazy." Sensing her intense investment in protecting her true self (Winnicott, 1965), I worried that the photo project had been too intrusive for her.

Home Instruction: A Bridge to the "Other-than-Mother" World

The New Year opened with mother's announcement that the Board of Education had approved home instruction. Ever superficially compliant, mother voiced her hope that J. would complete her high school diploma via home instruction and pursue a college education. J. shook her head vigorously to communicate that she did not share these educational aspirations but refused to provide a more nuanced perspective on this position. Mother clung desperately to her belief that "one day things will just fall into place." This belief impeded mother's openness both to fleshing out a roadmap towards change and to exploring her continued ambivalence about embarking on its path. In such moments, with the therapeutic alliance in ruins, I felt alone in the battle to enhance their capacity for self-refection.

Subsequent sessions were spent supporting the dyad's adjustment to the implementation of home instruction and, specifically, to the intrusion that the home instructor represented into their physical and psychological space. Mother described J.'s intense difficulty separating from her to meet alone with the female instructor, citing one occasion during which a screaming J. had had to be pried from mother's legs. Refusing to make eye contact with the instructor, J. wore a hooded top to obscure her face from the instructor's view. More disturbing were J.'s frantic pleas that mother locate an old ski mask to wear in the instructor's presence. This image felt akin to the emergence of psychotic process on the Rorschach as the patient's defenses collapse. Alarmed, I began to wonder whether her current symptom picture in fact warded off underlying psychosis and whether this fragile compromise formation represented her best level of adjustment. Certainly, her "panic tantrums" in response to enforced separation from mother and her attempts to retreat into "a quasi-stabilizing (secondary) autism" (Mahler et al., 1975, p. 293) with the ski-mask representing an attempt to erect a "frozen wall between the autistic child and the environment . . . to counteract the multitudinous complexities of external stimuli and inner excitations" (p. 289) felt reminiscent of Mahler's description of the prominent features of symbiotic infantile psychosis (Mahler, 1952). J. confirmed her sense that obscuring others from her view (just as she ducked to hide behind mother upon spying me at the clinic) obliterated their presence and the felt pressure to interact with them.

J.'s struggles were paralleled by mother's own ambivalence about relinquishing control and allowing J. to develop a relationship with an "other-than-mother" figure beyond her purview. This ambivalence was expressed through her frustration about the practical difficulties of home instruction such as its clashing with family mealtimes and the impediment it posed to mother working outside the home. Struggling to own her ambivalence, mother began to co-opt father's frustrations with the process, seemingly paving the way for the family's abandonment of the service. I worried that J.'s quiet efforts, namely, her completion of homework, would get lost in the midst of mother's vocal frustrations. Parent sessions thus highlighted J.'s efforts and the importance of having realistic expectations of the process, namely, the unlikelihood that J. would talk immediately, or even in the short term with the instructor, but rather seeing her gradual ability to tolerate this one-on-one relationship (like the therapeutic relationship) as a bridge to the world beyond the family. J.'s desire that class instruction take place "outside the home" where the instructor might be fatally hit by a car spoke to her own ambivalence about this new relationship.

The Ocean of Doom: Emergence of Aggression

Six months into the treatment, J. began to communicate through drawings initially completed outside of sessions and later during the therapeutic hour. At my request, mother had hesitantly completed a family drawing during a recent dyadic session, thereby seemingly granting her daughter tacit permission to express herself through this medium. Despite mother's comment, "I don't know how to make us look different," her drawing depicted the concrete signs of the dyad's progressive differentiation as seen in their now distinct styles of dress. Over time, J.'s drawings came to be accompanied by some minimal written expressive language in speech bubbles attached to her stick figure self-representations. She soon began to use drawing as a vehicle to express her murderous rage towards her parents. Like her banging, this long awaited symbolic representation of her rage injected renewed life both into the room and into supervision. Now, armed with her drawings, I could finally "show her" versus recount my experience of J. In fact, my supervisor shared that working from a relational psychodynamic perspective with the dyad had revived her own sense of possibility after her initial hopelessness upon hearing the case presented at the clinic the previous year.

J.'s own family drawing completed at home depicted J. as an angel among her minimally differentiated, zombie-like, devil-horned and tailed family. Her drawing seemed to speak to her sense of her family's emotional disfigurement and their intentions to use her for their own evil purposes. Their pimpled faces, as contrasted with her clear skin, suggested that it was they who were in the midst of the psychic restructuring of adolescence. Mother's visibly swollen belly was denied by J. to be carrying the baby that would enable her to escape the symbiotic tie with her mother. This emergence of J.'s aggression was paralleled by mother's increased comfort with contemplating her own hostile feelings as she expressed that she too should have been depicted in a halo given her years of accommodating to J.'s difficulties.

The first drawing completed in session depicted a smiling J. holding a gun in one hand and a knife dripping with blood in the other with a stick figure representation of her mother dead on the ground below, her eyes closed and her tongue hanging out her mouth. With mother now symbolically dead, J. was finally free to express herself through language (albeit written) for the first time in the treatment. The stick figure's "yeah" comment expressed J.'s triumph at destroying the bad part images of mother (described as "mean, dumb and aggravating" on the drawing) leaving unspoken J.'s yearning to hold onto her infantile tie with mother.

Just as we had wondered together about her other affective experiences, we now focused on exploring J.'s aggressive feelings towards mother with the aim of helping them feel "less terrifying" (Tuber & Caflisch, 2011). In an attempt to further differentiate the emotions underlying J.'s rage, the dyad was engaged in an adaptation of "The Anger Iceberg," an intervention I utilized in my work facilitating anger expression groups in juvenile detention. Mother (since J. declined) drew an iceberg and then generated behavioral indicators of J.'s anger (e.g., yelling, banging etc.) that were listed on the tip of the iceberg. Mother was then engaged in identifying the various emotional experiences that underlie anger (e.g., sadness, anxiety etc.) with the therapist wondering about additional potential experiences (e.g., feeling unsure about who one is, not feeling like I am my own person) that were added to the section of the iceberg below the ocean. J. agreed to circle the emotions she felt at home and bring them to the next session. Entitled "The Ocean of Doom," the embellished iceberg now included a gleeful J. kicking her screaming mother into the shark-infested water below to meet the same fate as father. J. had circled the words "unfair," "frustrated" and "disrespected." Taken together, her drawings appeared to speak to her intense murderous rage at being cast as the identified patient whose management excused her parents from participating in the feared outside world. From this perspective, J.'s silence could be understood as reflecting her angst about unleashing her seemingly limitless oral aggression against her family. However, I could not get mother to see her own contributions to this process. Rather, she could not be budged from her attribution of J.'s anger to increased parental limit setting around J.'s demands for material possessions (seen in the iPad J. clutched in the drawing) that had been a focus of recent parent sessions.

Towards Termination and the Potential Loss of J.'s Emerging Voice

With the end of our time-limited treatment three months hence, I began to worry that J. would lose her emerging voice. Guilt about abandoning J. coupled with my desire to see how the case evolved heightened my struggle to contemplate my own impending separation from the dyad. As we moved towards termination, mother's resistance to relinquishing the symbiotic tie she had fostered in J. seemed to only harden against the backdrop of the therapeutic progress J. had made. This progress included her increased communication through drawing and writing, her soft whispers to mother in my presence and her, albeit fleeting, eye contact with me. These incremental steps translated into behavioral changes outside of the treatment, specifically, her increased willingness to order at fast-food restaurants, respond to strangers' questions in stores and her continued, admittedly silent, participation in home instruction. There were also significant shifts within the family system such as father's resumption of part-time employment after reportedly being unable to work for the past several years due to needing to be home to manage J.'s behavior; and mother's sense that she and her husband, rather than J., were now "wearing the pants in the family." Furthermore, contrasting with her earlier desire to remain with mother forever, J. had recently shared her wish to adopt a huge dog that would provide protection in the perilous outside world she was now contemplating exploring.

Given the family's ongoing precarious financial situation and renewed threat of eviction, sessions with mother during this period shifted toward problem solving, identifying the barriers each family member currently had to working or attending school, while emphasizing the challenge of holding onto the importance of fostering long-term changes while in crisis.

As termination approached, sessions were utilized to validate the dyad's progress, explore their continued ambivalence about change and anticipate the challenges of transferring to a new therapist at the clinic. J. declined to communicate her experience of the treatment or termination. Mother focused on the practical implications of the transfer. As feared, I felt the physical and relational boundaries of the dyad's world shrinking as mother contemplated transferring to a clinic within walking distance of their home. In the final month of the treatment, with the family now awaiting eviction, I experienced a heightened sense of urgency. Feeling that I had nothing to lose and emboldened by my group supervision, I began articulating my conceptualization of the familial dynamics that maintained J.'s mutism and school refusal. Their blank stares in response underscored my sense of being alone in the treatment.

In our final session, J. endorsed her sense that mother, despite statements to the contrary, did not wish her to speak to non-nuclear family members, have friends or be out in the world. Mother expressed bewilderment at this disclosure. I was momentarily speechless. As they exited the therapy room, mother leading, J. gave me a playful backhanded wave goodbye. This seemed to both communicate the silent connection we had developed and, given its occurrence outside of her mother's view, to amplify J.'s disclosure of the felt maternal prohibition of "other-than-mother" relationships. While I understood that termination had created the conditions of safety for her disclosure, I longed for just one more session to explore the cliffhanger with which I had finally been entrusted. However, I also felt that this disclosure, and my sense that J. could now tolerate individual work, provided a strong platform upon which the next therapist could build. The last afternoon of my internship found me completing a lengthy treatment summary and photocopying the stack of supervision notes, journal articles and patient and parent drawings I had amassed in an attempt to preserve J.'s emerging voice for the next phase of her treatment. My anxiety, guilt and sense of abandonment around the termination were ameliorated with the transfer of J.'s case to Lauren DeMille, a fellow student from my doctoral program. The transfer to Lauren and our subsequent collaboration on this case has allowed me to follow the dyad on their therapeutic journey and delight in the intra-psychic and behavioral shifts that were simply unimaginable during my work with them.

For the most part, existing SM case studies conclude with the resolution of this symptom marking the success of the treatment. In reflecting on the process of writing this paper, I have grappled with what it means to write about a silent treatment of a selectively mute patient and my fears of exposing—perhaps further exacerbated as a therapist in training—what may be perceived as a failed treatment. On the basis of their clinical work with a nine-year-old selectively mute girl who remained silent for the duration of the treatment, Ruzicka and Sackin (1974) observe that, "while the total silence of the electively mute child can be a massive obstruction to the therapeutic process, effective treatment can be initiated and maintained, even though the child says nothing" (p. 552). I believe that the considerable intra-psychic and behavioral shifts exhibited by J. and her family and built upon in the next phase of the treatment with Lauren attest to the possibility for therapeutic progress in the absence of speech.

References

Atoynatan, T. H. (1986). Elective mutism: Involvement of the mother in the treatment of the child. *Child Psychiatry and Human Development*, 17, 15–27.

Bateman, A. & Fonagy, P. (2006). *Mentalization-based Treatment for Borderline Personality Disorder: A Practical Guide*. Oxford: Oxford University Press.

Blos, P. (1967). The second-individuation process of adolescence. *The Psychoanalytic Study of the Child*, 22, 162–186.

Browne, E., Wilson, V. & Laybourne, P. C. (1963). Diagnosis and treatment of elective mutism in children. *Journal of the American Academy of Child Psychiatry*, 2, 605–617.

Burlingham, D. T. (1945). The fantasy of having a twin. *The Psychoanalytic Study of the Child*, 1, 205–210.

Crenshaw, D. (2007). Play therapy with selective mutism: When Melissa speaks, everyone listens. *Play Therapy* (March), 20–21.

Freud, A. (1958). Adolescence. *The Psychoanalytic Study of the Child*, 13, 255–278.

Gaines, R. (2003). Therapist self-disclosure with children, adolescents and their parents. *Journal of Clinical Psychology*, 59, 569–580.

Hayden, T. L. (1981). Classification of elective mutism. *Journal of the American Academy of Child Psychiatry*, 19, 118–133.

Inoa Vazquez, C. & Myers, L. (2002). The case of Alicia: Understanding selective mutism and alopecia within a cultural framework. *Journal of Infant, Child and Adolescent Psychotherapy*, 2, 121–130.

Jacobsen, T. (1995). Case study: Is selective mutism a manifestation of dissociative identity disorder? *Journal of the American Academy of Child and Adolescent Psychiatry*, 34, 863–866.

Kaplan, S. L. & Escoll, P. (1973). Treatment of two silent adolescent girls. *Journal of the American Academy of Child Psychiatry*, 12, 59–71.

Lieberman, A., Silverman, R. & Pawl, J. (1999). Infant-parent psychotherapy: Core concepts and current approaches. In C. H. Zeanah (Ed.), *Handbook of Infant Mental Health*, pp. 472–485. New York: Guilford Press.

Mahler, M. (1952). On child psychosis and schizophrenia—autism and symbiotic infantile psychoses. *Psychoanalytic Study of the Child*, 7, 286–305.

Mahler, M., Pine, F. & Bergman, A. (1975). *The Psychological Birth of the Human Infant*. New York: Basic Books.

Meeks, J. E. & Bernet, W. (2005). *The Fragile Alliance: An Orientation to Psycho-therapy of the Adolescent* (Fifth Edition). Malabar, FL: Krieger Publishing.

Perl, E. (2008). The mother-daughter bond and its implications for understanding the therapeutic relationship. In *Psychotherapy with Adolescent Girls and Young Women*, pp. 13–39. New York: Guilford Press.

Pustrom, E. & Speers, R. W. (1964). Elective mutism in children. *Journal of the American Academy of Child Psychiatry*, 3, 287–297.

Ruzicka, B. B. & Sackin, H. D. (1974). Elective mutism: The impact of the patient's silent detachment upon the therapist. *Journal of the American Academy of Child Psychiatry*, 13, 551–561.

Sacks, O. (1986). Bound together in fantasy and crime (review of *The Silent Twins* by Marjorie Wallace). *New York Times Book Review*, October 19, pp. 3, 40.

Tatem, D. W. & Delcampo, R. L. (1995). Selective mutism in children: A structural family therapy approach to treatment. *Contemporary Family Therapy*, 17, 177–194.

Tuber, S.B. & Caflish, J. (2011). *Starting treatment with children and adolescents: A process-oriented guide for therapists*. New York: Routledge.

Wallace, M. (1987). *The Silent Twins*. New York: Prentice Hall Press.

Wassing, H. E. (1973). A case of prolonged elective mutism in an adolescent boy: On the nature of the condition and its residential treatment. *Acta Paedopsychiatrica: International Journal of Child and Adolescent Psychiatry*, 40, 75–96.

Winnicott, D. W. (1958). The capacity to be alone. *International Journal of Psycho-analysis*, 39, 416–420.

Winnicott, D. W. (1965). Ego distortion in terms of true and false self. *The Maturational Processes and the Facilitating Environment: Studies in the Theory of Emotional Development*, pp. 140–152. New York: International Universities Press Inc.

Winnicott, D. W. (1971). *Playing and Reality*. London: Tavistock.

Wright, H. L. (1968). A clinical study of children who refuse to talk in school. *Journal of the American Academy of Child Psychiatry*, 7, 603–617.

Youngerman, J. K. (1979). The syntax of silence: Electively mute therapy. *International Review of Psychoanalysis*, 6: 268–295.

10

PASSING THE BATON FROM ONE BEGINNING THERAPIST TO THE NEXT

An Adolescent Treated by Two Successive Interns

Lauren DeMille

Perhaps predictably, writing about a treatment in which the primary symptom is selective mutism (SM) at first left me speechless. With time, as I thought about my work with J., I began to find words to express what could often feel like an inchoate clinical process, and this brought momentary relief. Following on its heels, however, came a burgeoning sense of shame and an intense fear of exposure. I felt that each word I produced, each concept referenced, each clinical moment described would only highlight my incompetence and give fodder for others' more on-point interpretations or effective interventions. I felt as if I could not immerse myself in the task or assert my perspective, and I desperately wanted someone else to do the thinking and writing for me. Though these are common struggles and wishes for writers and beginning clinicians alike, the parallels to J.'s experience were obvious. She struggled to play and wanted her mother to be her voice.

This tidy concordant countertransference (Racker, 1957) though, does not end there. Not just indicators of J.'s experience, or common feelings for a beginning clinician, this fear of incompetence and the feeling of intense vulnerability also exist, I believe, in relation to the symptom of selective mutism (SM) in general (e.g. Youngerman, 1979). Lombard (quoted in an unattributed article, 2008) makes a distinction between mutism and silence, despite both referring to an absence of words. In her lexicon, silence in a session suggests possibility and an opening for exploration, while mutism regressively cuts off these potentials. This distinction captures the destructive quality of mutism, something that I felt clearly in the countertransference, and something J. would frequently enact or at times symbolize in our sessions. Bearing this destructive quality and staying engaged with it despite a desire at times to pull away came to feel like a central aspect of the treatment.

As a beginning therapist, I found J.'s silence in sessions to be particularly challenging both to treat and even to bear, dramatizing as it did the unknowability of others and a refusal to engage in a process that relies on engagement to have any hope of working. Her family's reluctance to reflect on itself and her symptom in relation to these familial dynamics amplified these experiences. Throughout this treatment I felt an obstinate stasis in the process as well as an unsettling instability. J. and her family system had maintained a view of the world as unsafe and inherited an intergenerational legacy of separation-individuation difficulties, making the stakes of symptom change seem especially high: things had to stay the same or they might fall apart. I was aware of receiving this message from both J. and her mother, each in their characteristic ways.

Transfer

In addition to receiving the transfer of J.'s case, I had also received Berko's formulation of it, which was enormously helpful. At the same time, I was somewhat intimidated by her understanding of the family and her connection to them. I wondered how I would find my own voice in the treatment, particularly with a family that I found so challenging and a symptom so unsettling. I wondered, too, how much J. would regress with the change of therapists, and how much this shift, that must have felt arbitrary to J., would stop the momentum of the family's work with Zoë, as well as support the family's unconscious goal that nothing should change. More fundamentally, what would Zoë "abandonment" of the family mean to them? And how might it confirm their wariness of others, including me?

Despite being somewhat intellectually prepared for my first session with J. and her mother, I was still amazed to see the dynamics I had held in my head playing out in the room. During my first session with J. and her mother—to which they arrived twenty minutes late, citing subway trouble—J. would not make eye contact with me, and instead closed her eyes during parts of the session as her mother and I spoke. When I noted J.'s shut eyes, her mother interpreted this as J. being "bored" with hearing familiar information yet again. I wondered aloud what it was like to begin work with a new therapist, and her mother made a comment about J. not liking to come to therapy, period, finding therapists' intrusions "weird." I was struck both by her mother's somewhat gleeful repetition of J.'s comment, and by this lack of acknowledgement of Berko in particular, when I believed that both J. and her mother likely had an intense connection to her. Clearly this erasure suggested a difficulty around bearing emotional experiences, particularly those around loss and separation. I fretted about my prospects for a future in this system, sensing J.'s mother's implicit challenge to me in the position of therapist: you, too, will be replaced. I wondered, too, how much she disavowed her own aggression towards treatment by piggybacking on J.'s. J.'s closed eyes clearly shutting me out caused me to feel both angry and insignificant.

They gave an indication of the primitive nature of the emotions involved, and the bluntness of defensive operations needed. It was as if the only way to get distance was to cut off or destroy. This tactic recalled that of the young infant who uses gaze aversion to self-regulate in the face of overstimulation (Beebe & Lachmann, 1994).

During this first session it was at first difficult for me to access spontaneous sympathy for J., but it emerged when I learned that her family was preparing to give up some or all of her pets to be ready for the eventuality of moving to her maternal grandmother's home, should they be evicted. J.'s father reconnected with his older brother, from whom he had been estranged, and was spending days at a time at his home several hours away. His tendency to separate in this way from the family was attributed to his being "independent." Where I thought there might be stated anger at his having left the family during this difficult time was instead a clear preference for his absence, as the house felt "calmer," due to the avoidance of conflict between the parents and to the absence of his loud voice and garrulous personality. In exploring life at home, J. was described as speaking often, frequently about somatic complaints and recently about wanting a "big dog."

In the next few sessions I learned more about this desire. Her mother enumerated all the impracticalities of getting a "big dog" now, as if she were pleading her case to J. In reaction to this logical argument, I tried to support an affective understanding of this wish. Unaware at this time that the family had voiced this wish to Berko, I seized on what was described as her incessant demand as a way into J.'s experience and desire. Her mother seemed to resist any symbolic exploration of what wanting a big dog might mean, and stayed in the realm of concrete (and legitimate) impracticalities. Internally, I noted her difficulty of attuning to the emotional resonance of this wish, and noted, too, my own frustration. I found myself identifying with J., wondering how her experiences and wishes were paved over with irrelevant and distancing talk, and felt my own desire to fall silent in frustration and rage. During this discussion, her mother happened to mention that J. had said that a "big dog" could "eat" her father. Hearing this, I pondered with her mother a connection between J.'s feelings towards her father, his recent return to the family home, and her intensifying demands for a big dog. I hoped to give voice to the message behind J.'s demands (which were being framed as irritating and irrational), in a sense rescuing and nurturing a communication that threatened to be lost. I also wanted to support J.'s mother in a parent role, and assess her comfort inhabiting such a position. In her mother's approach to these demands, and her explaining that in the past she had bought J. pets even while the family struggled financially, I sensed that J. was fed to placate her anger. Though it was the "food" J. asked for, it did not seem like what she truly wanted or needed, or was even truly demanding. I considered that her parents abdicated some power to J. in the name of not having to bear her intense affects or understand the emotional experiences that drove her demands, thus creating even more frustration as they insisted they tried to satisfy her.

The oral aggression towards her father was striking. In our fourth session, to my surprise, J. agreed to meet with me alone after a brief check-in with her mother. Sitting together with her in the office felt frightening and intimate, and I had to decide quickly how to spend this time, which seemed like a fragile and easily blundered opportunity. J. quickly closed her eyes after her mother left, leaving me feeling powerless and erased. I wanted to break the silence immediately, but decided to show J. that I could bear what she brought to sessions. Since her demands for a "big dog" were so far where I sensed her passion lay (besides in staying silent), I eventually spoke of my interest in this wish, and my sensing its intensity. She opened her eyes. She then declined engaging in any symbolic representations, such as drawing the big dog she imagined. Suddenly I felt aware of occupying a position that would become familiar: of demanding things from her, which she could then refuse. I was beginning to experience the almost paralyzing control that her symptom could exert over others, which has been described by others treating SM (e.g. Pichon-Riviere, 1958; Urwin, 2002) and the degree of vulnerability that such a need suggested.

Showing her a list of "feeling words," J. would not point to any herself but would nod or shake her head when I read some of them. She endorsed feeling "angry," "sad," "frustrated," and "loving" (the latter towards her pets). I determined that the first few feelings were in relation to her father and her unmet demand for a big dog. Through shaking her head, she denied that her father had hurt her, but rather that as her mother described he is "loud" and "annoying," and "riles up the little dog" that they already had. She nodded to indicate that she wished her mother could control her father better.

Dread

At this early stage of treatment, when her mother would report discussions she had with J. at home about, for instance, getting a big dog, J. would hit her mother's arm, which her mother normalized. She explained that J. often hit or flicked her, saying, "You hurt me, now I'll hurt you." In discussing this statement, J.'s mother said that she had no idea how she had hurt her, other than setting more limits lately. I found it impossible to elicit J.'s sense of hurt, and I suspected the hurt was terrifyingly unnameable. Not only was J. the recipient of her family's projections and its legacy of significant (though still vague) intergenerational difficulties, but I also felt a kind of "nameless dread" (Bion 1967, 1970) that she carried.

The degree of J.'s dread was significant. During an early session, J.'s mother casually referred to J. having daily panic attacks. Her casualness normalized them both because they were not unusual for her (and, in fact, she had panic attacks with varying degrees of frequency for years), and because they connected her to both her mother and grandmother, who also suffered from them. In another session, J.'s mother shared a dream J. had in which she was chased by pit bulls and saved by a German shepherd. J. would not engage around the dream and seemed embarrassed by her mother's report of it. We acknowledged the protection that a "big dog" could provide, including the comfort it would offer. It felt like a different kind of object.

Through our early sessions, we discussed themes of independence and dependency, and what these both looked like in their family. I had remembered J.'s father being described as "independent" for what sounded like (temporarily) abandoning the family during a stressful time. Through this example we discussed ways in which independence suggested a lack of concern for others and physical absence. In exploring J.'s mother's conscious hopes for her to have a "normal" life, I learned of J.'s desire to stay with her mother forever, represented in the image of pushing her mother's wheelchair when she was elderly. Illustrating their hostile-symbiotic tie with some humor, her mother added, "Yeah, down the stairs!" The hostility of their tie also of course held her mother's fears around what both independence and dependence could look like, namely vulnerability to destruction and abandonment.

Interventions with J.

In the midst of establishing our work together, I deliberated about the nature and goal of my interventions with J. Hers was such a striking symptom, and run through with such defiance; in talking's absence, I felt the desire to push for its presence. This dynamic was evident in her earlier behavioral treatment, which successfully produced speech in sessions but no real change. As is underscored repeatedly in the psychoanalytic SM literature (e.g. Kaplan & Escoll, 1973; Ambrosino and Alessi, 1979; Youngerman, 1979) I knew that the goal of treatment could not be to "get" J. to talk, and I tried to be mindful of this desire in myself.

I struggled with achieving a useful balance between dyadic and individual work. Like Berko, I was afraid of reinforcing symbiosis, but also did not want to pull J. and her mother apart prematurely, setting up therapy as another threat from the outside against which J. (and likely her mother) had to protect themselves, or creating such anxiety in J. that she would not engage. I wanted to make a space for J. to have her own voice and foster a chance of making a connection with her. At many times in our dyadic work, I felt that her mother's words filled the room, and the hour, and J. could fade away.

As I learned more about J. in dyadic sessions, I felt pulled to be J.'s voice, wanting to give words to what seemed like stark and frightening emotions that could only be managed by a solution that exacted such a high price. I caught glimpses of her intense affects, and the absence of a means to understand and metabolize them, leading her to discharge them physically, through screaming or in somatic complaints. Dyadic work on helping her mother mentalize J.'s experiences could often seem fruitless, which contributed to the pull to meet with J.

individually, for short amounts of time. During this portion of the sessions when her mother would leave, I spoke of what I had understood from our time with her mother, including such topics as the sadness and anger J. was feeling about having to give up her pets, her fear of the upcoming eviction and move to her grandmother's house, and her mother's mixed messages about independence. J. would engage through nodding or shaking her head, at times, while at other times closing her eyes and refusing to engage with me at all.

Holding on to our moments of communication, I later wondered if at times I overestimated J.'s desire to together find ways that she could express herself, or rather, I underestimated her terror and the degree of conflict around doing so. Yanof, in describing her treatment of a selectively mute child who, after making a connection with her, pulls away, writes "I quickly learned that, although words were not necessary for relating, the wish to communicate was" (Yanof, 1996, p. 84). What started as J. tolerating time alone with me in sessions (though often with her eyes closed for part of this time) eventually became an outright refusal to be alone in the office with me, at times shrieking when her mother left. I feared drawing us into a conflict around communication. I was torn between wanting to show her that she and I could both bear her anger and anxiety, and not wanting to enter a battle with her or dismiss her fear. After her mother left a session, she once had a tantrum in the office, kicking chairs and shrieking. I voiced how angry and scared she must be, and that I thought she was showing me how she felt like a little girl being left alone in a frightening place. J. then sat down with her back to me, still shaken. Through nods and head-shakes, she agreed that she wanted to stay a little girl, and that being an adult would be "boring." She also indicated that she wanted to stay with her mother forever. I said that therapy and my meeting alone with her probably seemed like I wanted to take her away from her mother, which elicited only a shrug.

In the next session she refused to enter the office at all, and sat on a cabinet in the hallway, refusing to engage. Her sit-in felt both punitive and like an expression of fearful avoidance.

Though acknowledging her fear, I wondered if I had mismanaged the emotional intensity that being alone with me had stirred. I also wondered if I had alienated J. Parallel to my conflict over balancing dyadic and individual sessions, I similarly felt a conflict between speech and silence. Perhaps my words were too impinging, or misattuned? Given J.'s stymied capacity for play and minimal engagement with me in sessions, I had not found a clear way into nonverbal communication with her. Since her communicative paradigm outside of the home involved silence in the presence of her mother, perhaps to enter it, dyadic work had to resume a central place in the treatment.

These several sessions of protest provided an opportunity to reflect, with her mother and J., on her fear of being without her mother, even in the therapy room. In discussing this difficulty, which J. endorsed through a nod (though this was hardly necessary), her mother spoke of J. wanting her to "be her voice." We considered reasons someone would want someone else to be their voice, focusing on anxiety and the need to circumscribe one's life (through oppositionality and silence) to manage it. We also considered the idea of not knowing what one's voice would be. Through focusing on her mother's anxieties about the world, we also continued exploring the closeness and security that came from her being J.'s voice. After refusing for several sessions or in between sessions to engage in any drawing, during this discussion, J. spontaneously drew a picture on the back of the clinic receipt. (I thought her choice of paper was noteworthy and highlighted how truly spontaneous her communication was, drawn not on the paper I had on hand in most sessions, but instead on a sheet of her choosing.) She wrote on the paper, "I wanna go home! now!" And then drew what she labeled as "two very mean and dumb people," namely, her father and grandmother, though I wondered if she also was referring to her mother and me. They were simple stick figure representations. After her mother and I saw her drawing, she then added herself strangling her father and grandmother, and throwing them off a mountain. She seemed pleased when I acknowledged the aggression in the drawing, smiling at me. With her anxiety more contained by her mother's presence, I thought that she could now symbolize her aggression rather than enact it physically, or fear that she would. I also wondered if now targeting her father and grandmother was a way of reaffirming the closeness to her mother that had been threatened, as well as displacing the rage she felt towards her.

Given the stress of a recent move into grandmother's home, I shifted the focus of sessions to support J. and her mother around this move, including some work with her mother on her relationship with her husband and mother.

Her mother described how unbearable it was to live with her own mother, including how she reminded J.'s family at every opportunity that their presence was bound to kill her. Described as a highly anxious woman, she experienced the family as a terrible intrusion, creating more and more rules to contain their unruly presence. Family members stayed in their individual rooms except to eat, but J.'s cat and other pets (such as a guinea pig and hamster) and the apparent lack of a plan for the family to get their own place still induced anxiety and resentment in the grandmother. I discussed the latter with J.'s mother, highlighting binds into which the family places each other for the sake of stasis and projecting blame: for example, J.'s father was not actively pursuing work, which provoked her grandmother, who then reacted punitively to the whole family, who then reacted with further helplessness. In discussing how conflict was manifest and handled, I learned that J.'s mother often deployed silence in both a passive-aggressive and a hopeless or exasperated way with her mother, suggesting that her words would have no effect. We could discuss the power of silence, and the place of both anger and despair from which it came, as well as J.'s identification with her mother's solution to handling her strong feelings. I saw an opportunity to explore with J.'s mother her own relationship with her mother, addressing the differentiation issues in treatment in a displaced, but still relevant, way.

While we were considering the power of silence, J.'s power in the family came into focus. J.'s tantrums at her grandmother's house led to her mother trying to control them, for fear that the grandmother would evict them to a homeless shelter. J. was in a terrible bind, both powerless to express her intense distress in any other way, but also with the responsibility of the family's fate in her hands in continuing this expression. J. acknowledged that her tantrums were effective in getting what she wanted (except for the big dog for which she still longed), and also a way of relieving her intense feelings. She brightened in a session when her mother said that in their previous apartment, J. could scream "as loud as she wants." I said that when she felt so much it must feel good to let it all out.

In fact, I felt growing frustration myself as J.'s mother spoke in sessions about her feeling overwhelmed by living with her own mother. While I offered support, I felt that attempts to explore dynamics or consider ways of communicating more effectively were dismissed. As with J.'s father, her mother would not include her grandmother in treatment, and I said that I understood the feeling that nothing would change. J.'s mother posed herself as victim to her mother's demands and unreasonableness, much as she posed herself vis à vis J.'s, but unwilling to work towards changes or appropriate assertiveness in response. She posed herself as similarly powerless with her husband. I tried to offer support in the face of her clear distress while also challenging her to identify and accept the clear anger she felt, and consider ways in which these dynamics could change. I now wondered if J.'s defiance and dramatic display of the futility of words were not only a sign of her holding disavowed aspects of her mother's experience, but also a way of demonstrating to her mother how to deal with "mean and dumb" people like her grandmother and father.

A Gift

I soon got another insight into J.'s anxiety around communication, with its potential for danger and shame. A fellow intern suggested that I get J. a small gift for her 18th birthday. I had been aware of her impending birthday for a while, but had not ever considered getting her a gift, perhaps sensitive about my position with her. I had some unexpected time before the session, and darted in and out of 99-cent stores, paralyzed even in this act of choosing a token gift. I was aware of the contradictory fears that a gift I chose would either displease her (either through the actual item chosen or the intrusiveness of the act) or have no impact, and I felt the imbalance in this fear disorienting. Rushing back to make our session in time, I popped into one more store, and saw an anime-style cat face on a keychain. The wide-eyed, frozen, smooth look of the cat's face reminded me of J.'s mien. I tried to relish the risk of my statement to her, rather than fear the shame of making a gesture.

Towards the end of the session, I presented the key chain to her, saying that 18th birthdays are important and should be marked. I explained that I had come to know that she loved cats, and that the keychain could one day hold a key to a home that felt more like her own, unlike her grandmother's house. (I did not add that a keychain, of course, also was a symbol of a child's independence, and being able to come and go without a parent. The flip side of the so-called "latchkey kid" also came to mind, with the air of neglect it contained.) J. gingerly accepted the gift, and looked at me with tentative curiosity. The silence between us felt full rather than voided.

Revisiting Photographic Communication

While I believe that it was important to discuss the substantial stress of living with J.'s grandmother and the feeling of insecurity it brought, I also felt J. fading away in these discussions, despite her substantial anger at her grandmother. I wanted to reengage her, but as was frequently the case, I was unsure of how. In thinking of nonverbal ways to connect, I remembered Berko's suggestion that J. take photographs with a disposable camera documenting her and her mother's world. Revisiting this activity several months later could provide its own snapshot of where in this world J. now was. I framed the activity as one that could help me understand what it was like to live with grandmother, acknowledging that J. had also taken pictures with Berko when things in her life were different. J. tentatively agreed to take the camera, and nonverbally engaged in a conversation about taking the photographs. With a sly smile, she indicated that she would not take photos of either her father or older sibling as their images might break the camera, which she indicated with her hand making an exploding sign near the camera lens. As in previous sessions, J.'s mother seemed to relish this aggression towards the other members of the household. We discussed how J.'s father and sibling were often critical of J. and her mother's handling of her, leading to her mother's defending herself and J. against criticism, disallowing her own more complex response to J.

   The photographs that she produced were taken entirely in her room at her grandmother's house. Her bedroom was extremely orderly, with pops of fluorescent pink flashing from the curtains and comforter. With its bright pink displayed dolls, and carefully arranged stuffed animals, the room struck me as that of a younger child. Most of the photographs featured J.'s pets, at times posed next to each other on her bed, sometimes adorned with pieces of cloth used to make hats and scarves. One photograph featured her mother sitting on J.'s bed, looking severe in a way I had not seen her in sessions; another was of J. holding her cat, beaming. As in the photographs she took several months ago, this relaxed and spirited presentation was one I had not seen. It was as if the photographs showed disallowed parts of both J. and her mother, parts that they each kept out of public view. J. seemed both shy and attentive to my response to the photographs, like a bashful toddler unsure of how her burgeoning self-assertion would be received. I admired her artistic flair with the photographs, experiencing her posed and costumed pets as a playful gesture. J. smiled at my appreciation.

Looking at the photographs later, I wondered how much she felt powerless like an animal caught in a flashbulb, or like one of her pristine dolls trapped in a box. I also sensed the control she had over these animals, and wondered if her treating them as her playthings also contained aggression and sadism. I wondered, too, if she had held me in mind as an audience for her creations. Her mother seemed surprised by some of the shots, which prompted a discussion of how J. took most of the photographs alone, in contrast to the previous photographic assignment. J. appeared attentive to her mother's response, too, which seemed like a mix of bemused appreciation and also suspicion, suggesting an anxiety (that she denied) over J. having some of her own world to represent. I shared my impression that J. was worried about her mother's response, perhaps not knowing if it was okay to have taken some photos on her own. Her mother insisted it was, while also emphasizing not knowing what would be on the film (though she said she was not surprised by the content). I said that J. now had the chance to share something with her, hoping to emphasize the satisfaction of such an exchange, in which some distance is required. We also acknowledged that these were the pets that J. would have to give up were the family to end up in a homeless shelter, and that her cat in particular was in an unstable position, her grandmother insisting that the family get rid of it as a condition of staying with her.

A striking aspect of the photographs, when taken in total, was the smallness of J.'s world. Whereas her previous shots were taken throughout her house and featured her sibling, these showed an even narrower world of her bedroom and pets, with one picture each of her mother and herself. I acknowledged the absence of her father and sibling from the photographs, and how they all were taken in her bedroom, which I said showed me how uncomfortable and unsafe she felt in the rest of her grandmother's house. This restriction was both a microcosm of her fears that kept her in the narrow world of the family, but also more broadly showed how her mutism suggested an internal world still too fragile to support her bridge to the outside world.

I then met alone with J. for a few minutes at the end of the session. She looked around the room in a way that felt more exploratory than avoidant, her eyes landing on the board game Clue. J. indicated liking this game, and agreed to play it with me in the next session. I wondered if we would, in fact, have any engagement of this sort, and found the idea both hard to believe and thrilling.

In the next session, J. would not play Clue with me, but eventually endorsed feeling "angry," "tired," and "bored." She often acknowledged this latter feeling, and I wondered how to explore it further. I treated boredom as if it was fascinating, and its nuances were something to be savored. During this discussion of boredom, and illustrating her need for her mother's physical presence, J. pointed to the door, signaling that she wanted her mother to come in. Eventually she joined the session. I had suggested drawing what was on their minds, and J. indicated that she would draw her own picture, but only if her mother did, too, and they each worked on their own picture. J.'s picture showed a dog and then a picture of one stick figure strangling another. When her mother and I tried to understand it, she took the picture away, writing "or" in between the two pictures, and we understood.

J.'s mother drew a picture of herself as "happy" and J. as "angry," with different styles of dress and different looks on their faces representing these emotions. In this split representation, each figure starkly displayed the emotions they unconsciously agreed to hold. In discussing the picture, it seemed that the difference in dress and emotional display belied a deeper enmeshment in which one could not live without the other, mother's happiness existing only in contrast to J.'s anger, and J.'s anger targeted at the Pollyannaish happiness of her mother. As if in response to this entanglement, J. concluded the session by aiming some of the weapons from Clue at her mother and smiling. Her aggression towards her mother (temporarily) relieved her of the burden of her alien self (Fonagy, Gergely, Jurist & Target, 2002), i.e. an aspect of her mother's mind that J. internalized, necessitating her mother's physical presence to receive as a projection.

I had not yet articulated to myself how dramatically the big dog was like a surrogate parent, the thing that J. was saying she needed to get to the next stage of development, offering stimulation, security, and exploratory companionship, as well as relating to her in a way free of its own projections.

As J.'s aggression persisted through the treatment, I began thinking more explicitly of Winnicott's concept of object usage (Winnicott, 1969).

I thought of J. as being stuck in the area that Winnicott describes between object relating and object use. If the object survives the child's attempts to destroy it in fantasy, their bond strengthens as the child's guilt over aggressive fantasies and behaviors is thereupon lessened. This bond paradoxically strengthens the separateness between child and object, as it implies the emergence of a private part of the self, a part that J. may not have robustly in her symbiotic tie to her mother, except at the cost of her mutism. Her wish for a big dog suggested a separate being that was available for her "use" and that would exist with her in a kind of harmonious rhythm, optimally distant. This image stood in contrast to a mother who felt both impinging and frightfully remote. J. could not yet use her mother as a separate entity to enhance her own separate identity, invigorating her for a connection to the world and other objects. I wondered about her own mother's ability to bear the destruction of which Winnicott speaks. This question is particularly important since "destruction" applies more to what must be borne by the object rather than what emanates from the subject. Winnicott explains, "The word 'destruction' is needed not because of the baby's impulse to destroy, but because of the object's liability not to survive" (1969, p. 714–715).

Change or Superficial Compliance?

I soon learned that the family would move to an apartment owned by an acquaintance, necessitating giving up J.'s cat, which I was surprised to learn had already happened. J.'s mother said that she handled it "well;" I did not know what to make of this. Her mother presented the move as an exciting and much-needed "push towards independence," saying that now her husband would have to maintain full-time employment and she would have to ensure that her part-time job gave her more hours. I feared that this situation was another in which change was expected to come from outside and I wondered how viable this new living situation would be. At the same time, I sensed some pride in her mother's demonstrating a move away from her own mother's home and towards the adult-hood that she acknowledged had remained elusive. She described years of living with J.'s paternal grandfather (which I had not heard of before), and how not being self-sufficient as a family was shameful. I expressed both my concern about this plan and my support for the efforts J.'s mother described to maintain it. But I wondered about this loss of the cat since our last session and the casual way in which J.'s mother mentioned it, including her suggesting that J. handled it "well." I met alone with J., who refused to write or draw anything as I acknowl-edged the loss of her cat, other than to write the cat's name, which I realized I did not know. When I mentioned that her mother had said she handled the situation "well," J. nodded, agreeing that she handled it differently than she would have a year ago. From a page of words that I wrote, J. pointed to "more accepting" to describe the difference, while also acknowledging being sad. I wondered if this acceptance was a mature coming to terms, or a hopeless resignation. In my won-dering with forced choices about the nature of her acceptance, she only shrugged her shoulders.

I felt sensitive to adopting the role of enforcer of compliance with unfortunate realities, where emotions would not be validated, but also wondered if in some small way acknowledging in sessions with her mother the sadness and anger at giving up her pets provided validation of these feelings that otherwise seemed to be dismissed. Perhaps acknowledging her emotional experience eased some of her potential protest and rage. J.'s overt acknowledgment of sadness, specifically, felt like an important shift. Though I viewed J. as depressed, this affect felt far from our sessions, including with her mother. J.'s willingness to experience and express some of this more vulnerable feeling with me suggested both growing trust in our relationship, as well as possibly a shift towards a depressive position, away from the paranoid-schizoid position of preoccupation with the survival of the self that she (and her family) so frequently occupied.

The theme of independence came up more explicitly in sessions now, often mentioned by J.'s mother. She said that she noticed that on the clinic receipt, J.'s marital status was listed as "single," prompting her to ask J., "Do you ever think this will say, 'Married?'" I had not heard her wonder about J.'s future before, other than to say that she might push her wheelchair (possibly down the stairs). I learned that J. had told her mother that she would never marry and instead wanted her mother to have a baby so that she could play with it (and as Berko has mentioned, perhaps divert the focus from her). We revisited her mother's conscious wishes for J.'s greater independence, and how they differed from J.'s own. During this session, J. pretended to sleep, and I remarked on her wanting something not to be happening. When we then met alone, she at first refused any kind of engagement, and I commented on her love of saying, "No," with which she agreed. I wondered if saying, "No" gave her a "charge," when she could otherwise feel quite bored and empty. She nodded her head, and also agreed that saying "No" and not speaking were "habits," but that she did not wish to break them.

Around this time, J.'s mother mentioned that she was no longer protesting about coming to therapy. Again, a development that seemed superficially like a marker of progress in a treatment where this could be so hard to discern could also be an indication of resignation and apathy. To use Winnicott's terms again, I feared that J. could be erecting a False Self to protect a True Self that she thought had no place in the treatment. Whereas she had previously more actively protested to keep this True Self safe, I wondered if now she resorted to superficial compliance. I had started noticing, though, that after sessions J. turned to look at me as she was walking away from the office, and we would hold eye contact briefly. This simple gesture gave me a bit of hope that she felt some curiosity about me and our connection. I had hastily explained my doubt in our connection as related to J.'s symptom: how could I discern any growth in our relationship in the absence of words, particularly when J. remained so oppositional? I again realized, though, that the presence or absence of speech is irrelevant to this assessment. Perhaps my doubt about our burgeoning connection was in part a protection against the fear of the intense affects that J. both brought to and tried to keep out of relationships, and an expression of the vulnerability that real connection implied.

Facing Danger

J.'s mother said that with the move to the new apartment J.'s demands for a "big dog" intensified. I focused again on the big dog as providing functions of differentiation, protection, and companionship, and her mother spoke first of her desire for J. to take a walk on her own to explore the neighborhood, and also the danger this posed. We explored her perceived danger in their safe neighborhood; that for instance J. might be harassed and would not be able to speak to defend herself. While highlighting her equating speech and the feeling of safety, I wondered at the likelihood of such harassment, with her mother saying that even a tiny risk was cause for concern. Her mother entertained the idea that adolescent boys might approach J., leaving her paralyzed with fear and vulnerability. Sexuality had never been discussed in the treatment, and now that it was, J.'s mother quickly erased it, saying with what seemed like some relief that J. had told her that she "doesn't like boys" with a "yet" implied. With these examples, we then revisited the paradox, addressed with varying degrees of directness throughout the treatment, that characterized her mother's wish for and communications to J.: that she should be more independent in a world that is not safe. In this discussion, her mother brought up a recent episode when J. was with both of her parents in a drug store. J. apparently wandered to a far part of the store to look at some items that interested her, causing her father to panic as if a toddler had run off, with mother questioning his concern. Her mother noted how it had been atypical for J. to wander off alone, and posed herself clearly against her husband's concern. I had not yet heard J.'s father described as occupying such a worried role, and this story gave me the opportunity to highlight the ambivalence the family felt about J.'s greater differentiation, with each parent alternately occupying split positions rather than both being able to hold the ambiguous complexity.

A Game of Catch

In my ongoing desire to engage J. nonverbally, but in a way that did not demand more engagement or ability to play than she had demonstrated, I often felt stumped. As with my difficulty purchasing a gift for J., I felt both devoid of expression and ashamed of any moves towards it. At times I struggled not to become as shut down as J. could be. I doubted that J. would start to engage with dolls or puppets, and I considered a less representational activity. I brought jars of Play-Doh to our next session, and wondered what might arise from this amorphous medium.

Meeting alone with J. towards the end of a session, I motioned towards the jars of Play-Doh, set on a table. She refused to move any closer, which did not surprise me. What did surprise me was that she did not shut her eyes, but instead rolled them. I was jolted by what I experienced as a moment of adolescent judgment of me and the juvenile activity I was suggesting. "What?" I asked, "Is Play-Doh for little kids?" She nodded vigorously. "For little kids? Like how old?" She shrugged, then held up five fingers. To me this was a wonderful and ridiculous moment: the 18 year-old who in many ways is a 2 year-old dismisses this activity as one for 5 year-olds. I knew that to lessen her fear and defiance I would have to playfully skirt them, but previous activities showed how difficult this was. The Play-Doh, however, provided a clear answer. I opened up a tub of Play-Doh, made a ball, and threw it towards her. Part of me expected her to let it fall to the ground as she shot me a withering look, but instead she caught it, and somewhat hesitantly, tossed it back to me. I then tossed the ball to her, and we continued this way for a few throws, I think to both of our surprise. It felt like this was a game played on the edge of uncertainty. My immersion in this game of catch quickly yielded to my wondering what would happen next, a thought I met with some anxiety. J. must have felt this, too, and she soon threw the ball on the ground next to me, off the precipice on which she and I were playing. I retrieved the ball and we picked up where we had left off. After a few more tosses, J. held onto the ball. She then smashed the ball between her hands, flattening it into a disc and jabbing holes in it with her finger. I felt attacked. I said that maybe she was frightened and now had to destroy anything between us. She stopped her destruction of the ball—or rather, her remaking of the ball into an inert and violated object. I said that maybe she had to keep me away because she thought I would destroy her relationship with her mother. She nodded. "It's so special, this closeness that you have." She nodded again. I said that maybe, though, sometimes closeness could feel overwhelming, making her angry and scared, and the only way to be safe was to destroy things. She then remade the punctured pancake into something resembling a cube, which she caressed between her fingers, apparently lost in this repetitive, tactile task. She seemed to be self-soothing and retreating into herself. I let the silence rest between us, a silence that in this moment felt more like one of erasure rather than silent communion. Eventually I spoke up, and J. showed me what she thought of my breaking the silence when she suddenly crafted the cube she had made into a dagger, looking at me with a mischievous smile. I laughed in appreciation of her gesture and said, "I guess you're telling me to stay away or someone might get hurt!"

Surprising Voices

Having not done so for a little while, J. feigned sleep in the next conjoint session. While her mother and I had in the past acknowledged the strangeness of speaking about J. as if she was not there, as J. became more of a presence in the room it came to seem particularly strange, and I suggested that she wait in the waiting room if she'd like. J. suddenly popped up, smiling, and softly but with enthusiasm said, "See ya!" as she bounded out of the room. Her voice sounded like that of a child. I asked her mother if this was J.'s typical voice, and she confirmed that it was, sharing her impression that J. was quite like a little girl, though she placed her age at 12, while I often experienced her as much younger.

I was, unsurprisingly, excited to hear J.'s voice in person,[1] and in what may have been a direct statement to me (in a unit with her mother). I experienced her rejection of me and her mother as somewhat playful. "See ya," of course, also dramatized themes in the treatment, as it is a farewell that suggests a reunion. Speaking with J.'s mother, I learned of her husband's violent temper, which she had not mentioned before in discussions of him. She denied any violence against family members, but said that he was prone to throwing things, wryly relating how many remote controls the family had to replace over the years. She disclosed an incident that happened at her mother's home when they were living there in which he threw a remote control that broke a piece of glass on an antique cabinet that J.'s mother then went to great lengths and expense to replace, hoping to create the impression that this had never happened. She likened J. to her father in terms of their angry displays. As with replacing the glass, her mother then seemed to cover up her statement, denying that any family members were afraid of him or the potential for escalating violence. Particularly in light of her continued adamant refusal to include him in treatment, I wondered what else was being omitted.

In this session, J.'s mother and I revisited her fears about J.'s increased independence. We discussed her fears of what might happen to J., and I wondered aloud about the likelihood of such imagined disasters and if the cost of the (illusive) belief that one could keep oneself completely safe was worth it. In this discussion, her mother suddenly said, "I guess I have to get over my own fears before she can get over hers." We both looked at each other, surprised. I felt as if someone else had made this statement, and J.'s mother said she had not had this thought before. She then spoke movingly of her wish for J. not to "get stuck" by what were her own fears, suggesting some differentiation between J. and herself.

Conclusion

I started this treatment knowing about Berko's fascination with the case but, myself, feeling quite alienated from J., her mother, and any sense of possible change or way to intervene. As termination approached with the end of my time at the clinic, I now understood Berko's urge to stay on at the clinic to continue working with the family. I initially myself felt quite struck dumb by the dramatic quality of J.'s symptom. Over the course of treatment, I came to differentiate J. from her striking diagnostic presentation, appreciating what seems like a wry, spunky side of her. Towards the end of treatment, she acknowledged that she believed she was a funny person. She similarly indicated that she wanted to be less angry and anxious than both her mother and grandmother. I found heartening her appreciation of humor and differentiated wishes for her emerging self. She also reported having fewer panic attacks and her mother noticed a decrease in her somatic complaints.

At the same time, J. was still firmly attached to her symptom in a family system that maintains it. With so much anger and aggression projected outward in this family's view of the world as dangerous, I knew that much more therapeutic work would be needed and many intense affects born to shift the system to one that could tolerate more differentiation among its members. At the time of termination, J.'s mother and father were sustaining the more "adult" life in which her mother expressed some pride. J. had indicated that her father's more steady work (on which her mother said she had insisted) made her feel "safer" as the threat of eviction lessened. I wondered how this greater safety might translate into tolerating more distance from her mother, a greater range of affects, and continuing early gestures towards engagement with a therapist. With termination imminent, I realized with disappointment that I would not know.

J.'s frustrated desire for a big dog remained a constant throughout the treatment, and I hoped to move an understanding of this wish into a symbolic realm, believing her wish expressed a desire for a different kind of connection, one that would enhance internal experiences of vitality, safety, comfort, stimulation, and closeness along with separateness. While her and her mother's ability or desire to understand this wish more symbolically remained somewhat thwarted, I felt as if in some register J. knew what she needed. To my amazement, as our treatment together was approaching its end, J.'s mother told me that J. had asked for her help in obtaining a non-driver's ID card so that she could volunteer at a nearby animal shelter. Her mother seemed to be helping her fulfill this wish. I bade them farewell after our last session, hoping that this wish, with its suggestion of a desire to invest in a world outside of that with her mother, could drive her in her next treatment.

My uncertainty as a beginning therapist along with the nature of J.'s symptom left me wishing for a concrete mark of progress as our treatment drew to a close. Part of developing as a therapist, I realized, was honing a way of questioning such wishes, as well as our ideas of where to look for signs of growth in our patients. Living with my work somewhere in the space between the poles of heroic transformation and paralyzing self-doubt felt like just as much of a challenge in this treatment as did finding ways of connecting with J. I realized, though, the impossibility of any true connection were I not to find such a place. I'd like to think that both J. and I progressed together towards finding our voices.

Notes

1 I had once heard her voice on a recording that she made at home, per my request. On the recording she repeated, "I want a big dog," and that she was "bored." She also made what sounded like a farting noise, which when I asked about in session she confirmed with a bashful smile, and causing me to laugh in appreciation.

References

Ambrosino, S. V. & Alessi, M. (1979). Elective mutism: Fixation and double bind. *The American Journal of Psychoanalysis*, 39, 251–256.

Beebe, B. & Lachmann, F. M. (1994). Representation and internalization in infancy: Three principles of salience. *Psychoanalytic Psychology*, 11, 127–165.

Bion, W. (1967). *Second Thoughts*. London: Heinemann.

Bion, W. (1970). *Attention and Interpretation*. London: Heinemann.

Fonagy, P., Gergely, G., Jurist, E., Target, M. (2002) *Affect Regulation, Mentalization, and the Development of the Self*. New York: Other Press.

Kaplan, S. & Escoll, P. (1973). Treatment of two silent adolescent girls. *Journal of the American Academy of Child & Adolescent Psychiatry*, 12(1), 59–72.

Lombard, P. (2008). The silence of the mother, or: Twenty years later. *Psychoanalytic Quarterly*, 77, 197–223.

Pichon-Riviere, A. (1958). Dentition, walking, and speech in relation to the depressive position. *International Journal of Psychoanalysis*, 39, 161–171.

Racker, H. (1957). The meaning and uses of countertransference. *Psychoanalytic Quarterly*, 26, 303–357.

Urwin, C. (2002). A psychoanalytic approach to language delay. *Journal of Child Psychotherapy*, 28, 73–93.

Winnicott, D. (1969). The use of an object. *International Journal of Psychoanalysis*, 50, 711–716.

Yanof, J. (1996). Language, communication and transference in child analysis. *Journal of the American Psychoanalytic Association*, 46, 79–117.

Youngerman, J. K. (1979). The syntax of silence: electively mute therapy. *International Review of Psychoanalysis*, 6, 283–296.

INDEX

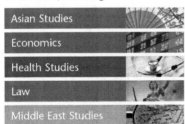

Printed by PGSTL